Sacred Sites and Repatriation

CONTEMPORARY NATIVE AMERICAN ISSUES

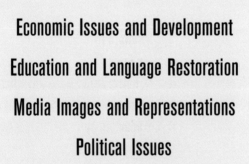

Economic Issues and Development

Education and Language Restoration

Media Images and Representations

Political Issues

Sacred Sites and Repatriation

Social Life and Issues

Sacred Sites and Repatriation

Joe Edward Watkins
Associate Professor of Anthropology,
University of New Mexico

Foreword by
Walter Echo-Hawk
Senior Staff Attorney, Native American Rights Fund

Introduction by
Paul Rosier
Assistant Professor of History, Villanova University

CHELSEA HOUSE
PUBLISHERS

T 31980

L

To Carol, who adds color to my personal and professional life in many different ways, and to my children, who continue to amaze me.

CHELSEA HOUSE PUBLISHERS

VP, New Product Development   Sally Cheney
Director of Production   Kim Shinners
Creative Manager   Takeshi Takahashi
Manufacturing Manager   Diann Grasse

Staff for SACRED SITES AND REPATRIATION

Executive Editor   Lee Marcott
Editor   Christian Green
Production Editor   Bonnie Cohen
Photo Editor   Sarah Bloom
Series and Cover Designer   Takeshi Takahashi
Layout   EJB Publishing Services

First Printing

9 8 7 6 5 4 3 2 1

Library of Congress Cataloging-in-Publication Data

Watkins, Joe, 1951-
  Sacred sites and repatriation / Joe Edward Watkins.
    p. cm. — (Contemporary Native American issues)
  Includes bibliographical references and index.
  ISBN 0-7910-7969-4
 1. Indians of North America—Material culture. 2. Indians of North America—
Antiquities—Law and legislation. 3. Cultural property—Repatriation—North
America. 4. Human remains (Archaeology)—Repatriation—North America. 5.
Cultural property—Law and legislation—North America. 6. Human remains
(Archaeology)—Law and legislation—North America. I. Title. II. Series.
  E98.M34W37 2004
  973.1'01—dc22
                        2004003266

Contents

Foreword

Walter Echo-Hawk

Native Americans share common aspirations, and a history and fate with indigenous people around the world. International law defines indigenous peoples as non-European populations who resided in lands colonized by Europeans before the colonists arrived. The United Nations estimates that approximately 300 million persons worldwide are variously known as tribal, Native, aboriginal, or indigenous. From 1492 to 1945, European nations competed to conquer, colonize, and Christianize the rest of the world. Indigenous peoples faced a difficult, life-altering experience, because colonization invariably meant the invasion of their homelands, appropriation of their lands, destruction of their habitats and ways of life, and sometimes genocide.

Though colonialism was repudiated and most colonies achieved independence, the circumstances of indigenous peoples has not improved in countries where newly independent nations adopted the preexisting colonial system for dealing with indigenous peoples. In such nations, colonial patterns still exist. The paramount challenge to human rights in these nations, including our own, is to find just ways to protect the human, political, cultural, and property rights of their indigenous people.

Contemporary issues, including those of culture, can be understood against the backdrop of colonialism and the closely related need to strengthen laws to protect indigenous rights. For example, colonists invariably retained close cultural ties to their distant homelands and rarely adopted their indigenous neighbors' values, cultures, or ways of looking at Mother Earth. Instead, they imposed their cultures, languages, and religions upon tribal people through the use of missionaries, schools, soldiers, and governments.

In the mid-1800s, U.S. government policymakers used the "Vanishing Red Man" theory, which was advanced by anthropologists at the time, as justification for the forcible removal of Native American tribes and for taking their lands. The policy did not work; America's indigenous peoples did not "vanish" as predicted. Native American tribes are still here despite suffering great difficulties since the arrival of Europeans, including an enormous loss of life and land brought on by disease, warfare, and genocide. Nonetheless, diverse groups survived, thrived, and continue to be an important part of American society.

Today, Native Americans depend on domestic law to protect their remaining cultural integrity but often that law is weak and ill-suited for the task, and sometimes does not exist at all. For example, U.S. federal law fails to protect indigenous holy places, even though other nations throughout the world take on the responsibility of protecting sacred sites within their borders. Congress is aware of this loophole in religious liberty but does not remedy it. Other laws promote assimilation, like the "English only" laws that infringe upon the right of Native Americans to retain their indigenous languages.

Another example concerns indigenous property rights. The *very* purpose of colonialism was to provide riches, property, and resources for European coffers. To that end, a massive one-way transfer of property from indigenous to nonindigenous hands occurred in most colonies. This included land, natural resources, and personal property (called *artifacts* by anthropologists). Even dead bodies (called *specimens* or *archaeological resources* by anthropologists) were dug up and carried away. The appropriation has been extended to intellectual property: aboriginal plant and animal knowledge patented by corporations; tribal names, art, and symbols converted into trademarks; and religious beliefs and practices *borrowed* by members of the New Age movement. Even tribal identities have been taken by "wannabes" masquerading as Native Americans for personal, professional, or commercial gain. In beleaguered Native eyes, little else is left to take. Native legal efforts attempt to stem and reverse this one-way transfer of property and protect what little remains.

Through it all, Native American tribes have played an important role in the American political system. The U.S. Constitution describes the political relationships among the federal government, states, Native American tribes, and foreign nations. Hundreds of tribal governments comprise our political system as "domestic dependent nations." They exercise power over Native American reservations, provide for their tribal citizens, engage in economic development, and sometimes come into conflict with states over intergovernmental disputes. Many tribes own and manage vast tracts of tribal land, extensive water rights, and other natural resources. The United States holds legal title to this property in trust. As trustee, the United States exercises significant power over the lives of Native Americans and their communities; and it is responsible for their well-being. These "nations within nations" are not found on international maps and are invisible to many in our own country.

Prior to 1900, about five hundred treaties between Native American tribes and the United States were duly ratified by the Senate and signed into law by the president. Treaties contain hard-fought agreements that were earned on American battlefields and made between Native American tribes and the United States. They opened vast expanses of Native American land to white settlement, protected remaining Native property, and created the political relationships with the U.S. government that remain to this day. As President George H.W. Bush said during his inaugural address in 1989, "great nations like great men must keep their word." Though many treaties were broken, many promises are honored by the United States today and upheld by federal courts.

The history, heritage, and aspirations of Native Americans create many challenges today. Concern for tribal sovereignty, self-determination, and cultural survival are familiar among Native Americans. Their struggles to protect treaty rights (such as hunting, fishing, and gathering rights), achieve freedom of religion, and protect Mother Earth (including land, resources, and habitat) are commonplace challenges, and sometimes include the task of repatriating dead relatives from museums. Each year, Congress passes laws affecting vital Native interests and the Supreme Court decides crucial cases. The hardships that Native Americans have endured to keep their identity are little known to many Americans. From the times of Red Cloud, Seattle, and Chief Joseph, Native leaders have fought to achieve these freedoms for their people. These ideals even today motivate many Native American soldiers to fight for our country in distant lands, like Iraq and Afghanistan, with the hope that the principles fought for abroad will be granted to their relatives at home.

Today, vibrant Native American communities make significant contributions to our rich national heritage. Evidence of this can be found in the recently opened National Museum of the American Indian, in Washington, D.C. It is also found throughout the pages of *Native Peoples* magazine and other Native media. It fills the best galleries, museums, and auction houses. It can be seen in the art, dance, music, philosophy, religion, literature, and film made by Native Americans, which rank among the world's finest. Visitors crowd tribal casinos and other enterprises that dot Native American reservations in growing numbers. Tribal governments, courts, and agencies are more sophisticated than ever before. Native American-controlled schools and colleges are restoring the importance of culture, traditions, and elders in education, and instill Native pride in students. The determination to retain indigenous cultures can be seen through the resurgence of tribal language, culture, and religious ceremonial life.

Yet many old problems persist. Too many Native Americans are impoverished and in poor health; living at the very bottom of almost all socioeconomic indicators and often in violence-ridden communities where disease, such as AIDS, knows no racial or cultural boundaries. Some socioeconomic problems stem from the aftermath of colonization of Native lands, peoples, and resources, or from efforts to stamp out Native culture and religion. Others stem from prejudice and hostility against Native people that has long characterized race relations in the United States.

As our nation matures, we must reject, once and for all, harmful policies and notions of assimilation and ethnocentrism, and embrace cultural relativism in our relations with the Native peoples who comprise our diverse society. History teaches where racial stereotypes, myths, and fictions prevail, human rights violations soon follow. But social change comes slowly and ethnocentrism remains deeply rooted in mass media and other corners of society. To little avail, Native people have told Hollywood to stop stereotyping Native Americans, protested against harmful racial stereotypes used by groups like the "Redskin" football team, and requested appropriate coverage of Native issues by the mainstream media. Native life is far different than how it has been depicted in the movies and by school and professional mascots.

Regrettably, schools do not teach us about Native Americans; textbooks largely ignore the subject. Sidebar information is provided only when Pilgrims or other American heroes are discussed, but Native Americans mostly "disappear" after dining with Pilgrims, leaving students to wonder about their fate. As a result, the people who met Columbus, Coronado, Custer, and Lewis and Clark are still here, but remain a mystery to legislators, policymakers, and judges who decide vital Native interests. Those interests are too often overlooked, marginalized, or subordinated by the rest of society. The widespread lack of education and information is the most serious problem confronting America's Native people today.

CONTEMPORARY NATIVE AMERICAN ISSUES will help remedy the information gap and enable youth to better understand the issues mentioned above. We are fortunate to have comprehensive data compiled in this series for students. Armed with facts, this generation can address Native American challenges justly.

Walter R. Echo-Hawk
Boulder, Colorado
March 2005

Introduction

Paul Rosier

During the mid-1970s, I attended Swarthmore High School in suburban Philadelphia, Pennsylvania. There, I learned little about Native Americans other than that they had lived in teepees, hunted buffalo, and faced great hardships in adapting to modern life at the end of the nineteenth century. But I learned nothing about Native Americans' experiences in the twentieth century. And as a member of the Tomahawks, the high school football team, I was constantly reminded that Native Americans had been violent and had used primitive weapons like tomahawks. Movies and television shows reinforced these notions in my young and impressionable mind.

It is my experience from teaching Native American history at the university level that students in middle and high schools across the country, have not, with some exceptions, learned much more about Native Americans in the twentieth century than I did thirty years ago. Several years ago, one of my students asked me if Native Americans still live in tepees. He and many others like him continue to be presented with a limited and biased interpretation of Native Americans, largely from popular culture, especially sports, where professional teams, such as the Washington Redskins, and mascots, such as the University of Illinois' Chief Illiniwek, continue to portray Native Americans as historical objects, not as citizens of this nation and as members of distinct tribal communities.

In 1990, President George H.W. Bush approved a joint resolution of Congress that designated November National Indian Heritage Month, and over the following years similar proclamations were made by presidents William J. Clinton and George W. Bush. On November 1, 1997, President Clinton stated: "As we enter the next millennium we have an exciting opportunity to open a new era of understanding, cooperation, and respect among all of America's people. We must work together to tear down the walls of separation and mistrust and build a strong foundation for the future." In November 2001, President Bush echoed Clinton by saying, "I call on all Americans to learn more about the history and heritage of the Native peoples of this great land. Such actions reaffirm our appreciation and respect for their traditions and way of life and can help to preserve an important part of our culture for generations yet to come."

We still have work to do to further "understanding, cooperation, and respect among all of America's people" and to "learn more about the history and heritage of the Native peoples of this great land." The information presented in CONTEMPORARY NATIVE AMERICAN ISSUES is designed to address the challenges set forth by presidents Clinton and Bush, and debunk the inaccurate perceptions of Native Americans that stretches back to our nation's founding and continues today. For example, schoolchildren's first intellectual exposure to Native Americans may well be through the Declaration of Independence, which describes Native Americans as "merciless Indian savages, whose known rule of warfare is an undistinguished destruction of all ages, sexes, and conditions."

The series' authors are scholars who have studied and written about the issues that affect today's Native Americans. Each scholar committed to write for this series because they share my belief that educating our youth about Native Americans should begin earlier in our schools and that the subject matter should be presented accurately.

Outside the classroom, young students' first visual exposure to Native Americans likely comes from sporting contests or in popular culture. First impressions matter. C. Richard King, Associate Professor of Comparative Ethnic Studies at Washington State University, discusses this important issue in his volume, *Media Images and Representations*. King looks at how these early impressions of Native Americans persist in film and television, journalism, sports mascots, indigenous media, and the internet. But he also looks at how Native Americans themselves have protested these images and tried to create new ones that more accurately reflect their history, heritage, and contemporary attitudes.

In *Education and Language Restoration*, Jon Allan Reyhner examines the history of how Native Americans have been educated in boarding schools or mission schools to become assimilated into mainstream American society. Reyhner, Professor of Education at Northern Arizona University, considers how Native Americans have recently created educational systems to give students the opportunity to learn about their culture and to revitalize dormant languages. Like non-Native American students, Native students should invest time and energy in learning about Native American culture and history.

This educational process is important to help Native Americans deal with a myriad of social problems that affects many communities in our country. In their volume *Social Life and Issues*, Roe W. Bubar and Irene S. Vernon, professors at the Center for Applied Studies in American Ethnicity at Colorado State University, review the various social issues that Native Americans face, including health problems like AIDS and alcoholism. They also consider how Native American communities try to resolve these social and health crises by using traditional healing ceremonies and religious practices that are hundreds of years old.

One very important issue that has helped Native American communities heal is repatriation. Joe Edward Watkins, Associate Professor of Anthropology at the University of New Mexico, examines this significant matter in his volume, *Sacred Sites and Repatriation*. Repatriation involves the process of the government returning to individual tribes the remains of ancestors stolen from graves in the nineteenth century, as well as pots and ceremonial objects also taken from graves or stolen from reservations. Native Americans have fought for the return of objects and remains but also to protect sacred sites from being developed. Such places have religious or spiritual meaning and their protection is important to ensure continued practice of traditional ceremonies that allow Native Americans to address the social and health problems that Vernon and Bubar describe.

In *Political Issues*, Deborah Welch, the Director of the Public History Program and Associate Professor of History at Longwood University, writes about how Native Americans reclaimed political power and used it to strengthen their communities through legislation that promoted both repatriation and the protection of sacred sites, as well as their ability to practice their religion and traditions, which the federal government had prohibited into the 1970s. Native American tribal communities have fought for their sovereignty for decades. Sovereignty means that tribal governments set the rules and regulations for living within reservation boundaries. Federally recognized tribal groups maintain their own courts to prosecute crimes—with the exception of major crimes, that is, rape, arson, and murder. Native Americans living on their own reservations generally do not need to obey state regulations pertaining to hunting and fishing and do not pay state income or excise taxes, though they are responsible for paying federal income taxes.

Tribal governments also help to create economic opportunities for their people, the subject of Deborah Welch's second volume, *Economic Issues and Development*. In this book, Welch examines the ways in which Native Americans have tried to create employment in businesses, which include ranching, mining, golf resorts, and casinos. She also considers how Native Americans have tried to develop projects within the context of their environmental traditions. As with other elements of their lives, Native Americans try to use their tribal histories and ceremonies to confront the economic challenges of modern life; to prosper by being *both* Native and American, while ensuring the health of Mother Earth.

Limited coverage of Native American life in schools, newspapers, and broadcast media has helped to perpetuate Americans' stereotypical views of Native Americans as either wealthy from gambling or suffering from poverty and alcoholism. The real picture is not so easy to paint and involves more than 560 separate Native American nations within the United States, which includes 4.1 million people who identify themselves as solely or in part Native American. The goal of this series is to explore the many different dimensions of the complex world of today's Native Americans, who are divided by geography, politics, traditions, goals, and even by what they want to be called, Native American or American Indian. Most Native Americans, however, prefer to be identified by their tribal name, for example, Lakota (Sioux), Blackfeet, or Diné (Navajo). And yet Native Americans are some of the most patriotic Americans, in part because their ancestors and relatives have died fighting in the name of freedom, a freedom that has allowed them to be both Native and American. As U.S. Army Sergeant Leonard Gouge of the Oklahoma Muscogee Creek community put it shortly after the September 11 attacks, "By supporting the American way of life, I am preserving the Indian way of life."

Paul Rosier
Villanova, Pennsylvania
March 2005

1

Introduction to Repatriation Issues

Think about your earliest memories of Thanksgiving. Remember the stories of how the Pilgrims, starving that very first winter in America, were saved by the Indians? Remember the story of Squanto, the Indian who taught the Pilgrims how to plant corn kernels and to use fish as fertilizer to make the corn grow better? If you remember those stories, you will realize how great a role American Indians played in helping the Pilgrims to survive and flourish.

But there are other stories that are rarely told. These tell about how some of the Pilgrim explorers, soon after arriving in their new land, happened upon a grave. They dug into it and found the bones and skull of a man and the bones and skull of a small child, along with some cultural objects that had been placed with the bodies. One of the discoverers wrote that they took some of the prettiest things away and covered up the bones again. By November 19, 1620, only eight days after the Pilgrims had first anchored off eastern

Massachusetts, American Indian graves had already been plundered for their contents.

Of course, grave robbers and looters are not the only people who are interested in the things left behind by early populations of North America. Anthropologists and archaeologists often collect bits and pieces of items left behind by inhabitants (called artifacts) as part of their research. These materials, when studied by scientists, provide information that helps them to better understand the cultures that lived in North America before the Europeans arrived. Museums also view the preservation of objects from the past as a part of their duty, because those items can be used to help teach people about all the different cultures that once existed or that currently exist in the world.

American Indian human remains and cultural items have been taken from Indian people ever since the founding of the English colonies in North America, and the practice continued on through the eighteenth and nineteenth centuries. In the 1840s, for example, Dr. Samuel Morton, an American physician, tried to prove through skull measurements that the American Indian was racially inferior to non-Indian U.S. citizens and was therefore doomed to die out as a culture. The skulls Morton needed for his comparative "cranial library" were American Indian skulls gathered by Indian agents, physicians, grave robbers, and military personnel. These people took the skulls from old and recent graves of tribes defeated in battles. Sometimes they even took Indian remains from the battlefields almost immediately after the fighting had ended. Additionally, in 1868, the surgeon general of the U.S. Army ordered army personnel to collect Indian crania and other body parts for the Army Medical Museum to be used for comparative material and for scientific study.

Not everyone in the United States believes that museums and similar places should keep and study skeletons and other types of artifacts. Many American Indian tribes, families, and

In 1989 and '90, Congress passed two laws—the National Museum of the American Indian Act and the Native American Graves Protection and Repatriation Act—that required museums to return sacred items to American Indians. Shown here is Eugene C. Ryan, a chief of the Cheyenne River Sioux, who is being presented with a Ghost Dance shirt that had been on display at the Kelvingrove Museum in Glasgow, Scotland.

individuals want museums to give human skeletal remains and special cultural objects back to the people to whom they once belonged so that tribes can ceremoniously rebury the human remains or reintroduce the sacred objects as part of their traditional religious practices.

In 1989 and 1990, Congress enacted laws that required museums that receive any federal money to identify skeletons, bones, funerary items, and sacred objects within their collections that once belonged to American Indians. The laws also required museums to return the items to the tribes if the tribes could prove that the objects belonged to them and if the tribes wanted them back. But scientists and other people who work with and study these special items complained that, if the items are returned, science could lose valuable information about how humans have adapted throughout history.

The process of returning human remains and other special classes of cultural objects has gone on for nearly fifteen years. It has not been totally smooth in its operation, and not as many cultural objects and sets of human remains have been returned as many tribes have expected. Still, the return process has begun.

But human remains and important cultural objects are not the only concerns that American Indians have in relation to their right to continue to practice their traditional culture. As a result of the various treaties signed by the tribes, they were often forced to move away from areas where they had lived before the Europeans arrived. After they moved, American Indians learned where game could be found in their new homelands, which plants would grow best in the new soils and climates, and how to adapt their lifestyles to the changing seasons. They were not, however, able to visit the sacred sites they needed for the free practice of their religion without hardship or risk.

The First Amendment of the Constitution guarantees all American citizens the right to the free practice of their religion. American Indians, however, have had to fight for that right as much as (if not more) than any other ethnic group in the United States.

At one time, the practice of Native religious ceremonies, such as the Sun Dance, was outlawed, and anyone participating in such rites could be put in jail. Things have changed in that respect, but there is another aspect of traditional religion that continues to be a concern among tribal participants.

Certain landscapes or places are an important part of many traditional Indian religions and have been used for generations. Tribal members go to these places to communicate with a higher spirit. Particular sites on the landscape may be considered sacred to members of a tribe because of their connection to tribal stories or histories.

Many of these places, however, are located in areas where the tribe originally lived but are no longer easily accessible to all tribal members. Some places are now part of what is considered to be private property. Additionally, because some of these sacred sites exist within distinctive formations or landscapes, many are now inside state or federal parks.

American Indians have argued that not allowing tribal members to visit these special sites is the same as not allowing a Christian to visit a church, a Jewish person to visit a temple, or a Muslim to visit a mosque. Although there have been attempts by the federal government to address the issue of access to sacred sites, many traditional tribal leaders feel more should be done.

2

Why Is There Conflict and What Is Repatriation?

*We resist the categorization of our ancestors' remains as
"archaeological populations," because it negates
our ability and right to define or ascribe our
own peoples based upon our own history, customs
and values. . . . They are simply our ancestors,
and they, too, deserve the self-evident human right
to rest in peace, no matter where they lived,
when they lived or died, or their questionable value to science.*[1]
—Tex G. Hall, chairman, Three Affiliated Tribes
of the Fort Berthold Indian Reservation

You may have seen some of the older Western movies, where cowboys are fighting a group of Indians, and someone says, "The only good Indian is a dead Indian." Well, that was the attitude of whites throughout much of the 1800s, when the pioneers were crossing the

Great Plains on their way to Washington, Oregon, and California. American Indians who lived in the Great Plains area and who fought to protect their land were seen as an obstacle to the United States' westward growth and as people who stood in the way of progress.

U.S. government programs aimed at helping the westward expansion across the continent stood in direct conflict with programs that were meant to keep the Indians separated from the American public. Treaties with Indians were meant to limit not only the movements of the tribes but also to restrict the interaction between non-Indians and the tribes. It was the U.S. government's intent to leave the Indians with tracts of land where they could live and hunt without being bothered by outsiders. As settlers continued to move west, however, the demand for Indian land grew until conflict was inevitable.

Because of the general belief that American Indians were doomed and that their so-called primitive culture was about to disappear, anthropologists of the time believed it was their job to record as much of the Indians' culture as possible before it was lost. Anthropologists studied Indian tribes and wrote about their lifestyles, and they were soon viewed as the experts when it came to Indian issues.

Anthropology in its broadest sense is the comprehensive study of humankind that compares human cultures by looking at the ways various human groups are different from one another. It is made up of four subfields that examine particular aspects of human populations: *Archaeology* studies the cultures and materials from human groups of the past, while *biological* (or *physical*) *anthropology* examines the biological and physical nature of the human body. *Cultural anthropology* studies humankind as a social organism and looks at the way people have used tools and customs to adapt to their environment, and *linguistic anthropology* specializes in the study of human languages throughout the world.

A number of modern anthropologists have traced the history of anthropology's relationship with Indians, and many have indicated that early American attitudes had a tremendous amount of influence not only on the manner in which the federal government treated Indians but also on the way anthropologists have studied and portrayed them. One anthropologist, Bruce Trigger, believes that the conclusions scientists reach are influenced a great deal by the attitudes and opinions that are common in the societies in which they live.

THE MOUND BUILDER CONTROVERSY

A good example of the scientific thoughts about Indian cultural development in North America revolved around what has been called the "Mound Builder controversy." "Mound Builders" were believed to have been a non-Indian race of people, perhaps related to the prehistoric Mexicans, Danes, or even Hindus, who had either moved away from eastern North America or had been wiped out by the Indians. Most scientists of that time felt that the Indians of North America who were living in the United States at the time were not capable of making the mounds found in eastern North America, and, therefore, there obviously had to have been another, earlier race of non-Indians who had built the enormous mounds.

One individual who was interested in the origins of the burial mounds was Thomas Jefferson, the third president of the United States. In 1784, when he was the chairman of a committee studying how the Western lands should be governed, he carefully excavated a long, narrow trench through a burial mound in order to find out how it had been constructed. He found that human bones had been deposited on the ground and then covered up with earth. The process had been repeated so many times that the mound eventually reached a height of nearly twelve feet. Despite his discovery, Jefferson did not participate in the Mound Builder controversy; instead, he apparently chose to wait until there was more proof of the mounds'

The Etowah Indian Mounds in Georgia are thought to be built by early American Indians known as Mound Builders. Many scientists in the eighteenth century thought that American Indians were not capable of building such complex architectural structures and hypothesized that they were instead built by prehistoric Mexicans, Danes, or even Hindus.

purpose and history before publicly saying anything about the possible origins and ultimate fate of the people who had built the mounds.

Numerous explorers and travelers encountered, recorded, and wrote about the mounds in eastern America throughout the 1800s, eventually reaching the conclusion that there had been no "Mound Builder" race, but that the mounds had been built by earlier groups of American Indians. By the time archaeologists finally proved that the mounds were products of the ancestors of the Indians living in the late nineteenth century, most Indians had been forcibly moved away from their original homelands and pushed westward into places like Indian Territory (later to become the State of Oklahoma).

When scientists finally abandoned the idea of the lost Mound Builder race in 1894, however, it had very little effect on the negative attitudes of the general population toward the American Indian. The Indians were still considered savages, destined to vanish from the earth in the face of the movement of white civilization across the North American continent.

Today's anthropologists, looking back on the controversy, realize that it was more than just a debate among scholars. Some people argue that the extermination of American Indians by westward-moving U.S. settlements was somehow morally easier for the U.S. government to justify if the Indians were considered more "primitive" than white Americans. Other scholars believed that the Mound Builder controversy might have served the political administrations well as an excuse for exterminating the Indian groups that had destroyed North America's only "civilized" culture.

Conversely, other anthropologists argue that the archaeologists who worked to prove the Indians were the descendants of the people who built the mounds stood up for the Indians in opposition to their own culture. They helped American Indians by proving scientifically that Indians were more accomplished than many had perceived them to be during a time when Americans were carrying on wars against them and when the stereotype of the savage Indian was a common way to make it easier for whites to kill Indians or force them to move.

THE U.S. GOVERNMENT'S RELATIONSHIP WITH AMERICAN INDIANS

In the 1930s, the U.S. government tried to change the structure of its relationship with American Indians. The Wheeler-Howard Act, better known as the Indian Reorganization Act of 1934, encouraged the creation of tribal councils and constitutions in an attempt to allow American Indians to rule themselves, to change the existing injustices on the reservations, and to place them on the road to "progress." Some advancement toward establishing better tribal control of their affairs was made, but a new policy came into being that seemed to stop that forward movement.

In 1953, with the passage of House Current Resolution 108, Congress indicated its intent to "terminate" federal relations with tribes and to pressure Indians to assimilate into mainstream American society. This act, in effect, simply would have allowed the U.S. government to ignore all the treaties it had previously entered into with the Indian tribes. This proposed program met with resistance from the tribes and finally, in 1958, the U.S. government ceased trying to terminate Indian tribes and instead reinstated programs aimed at providing care and support to them.

While all these governmental programs aimed at changing the U.S. relationship with the tribes were being put forth, social unrest among minority cultures in the United States was growing. The 1950s and 1960s were a time of social and political unrest, especially in the area of civil rights. African American populations in the South worked to increase the amount of freedom that black citizens were able to exercise. Through their efforts, voting laws were changed and social and governmental policies that had acted to segregate African Americans and whites were examined and altered. However, because of long-standing tensions between the races, quiet protests often erupted into violent clashes that involved police, protesters, and even innocent bystanders.

Also during the 1960s, the "Pan-Indian" movement began. It identified the problems of any American Indian group as a matter of concern for all living American Indian groups. This attitude reflected a new political consciousness, and groups of non-related Indians began to work together for the perceived benefit of all Indians.

CONFLICT BETWEEN ANTHROPOLOGISTS AND AMERICAN INDIANS

With the growing political and social changes occurring in "Indian Country" came a similar change in the ways that

American Indians related to scientists and people who studied them. Proponents of Native unity were seen as a threat by many anthropologists who sometimes felt American Indians were attempting to restrict the anthropologists' freedom to carry out research. The idea that anthropologists have a right to access cultural material because their research is aimed at producing knowledge for the public benefit is in apparent conflict with the beliefs held by most American Indian groups. According to these Indians, cultural material remains the property of the descendants of the people who produced it—not the property of whomever or whatever organization owns the land where the material is found.

Anthropologists who once enjoyed amiable relationships with particular tribal groups were dismayed to find that new political groups such as the American Indian Movement (AIM) were trying to initiate changes in the way research was done. These organizations, made up of individuals from many different tribes rather than representatives of just a single tribe, used protests and other militant actions to make their points.

An analysis of American Indian protests during the decade from 1969 through 1979 shows that American Indians viewed anthropologists with suspicion. The social scientists were perceived as a threat to American Indian ancestors and their skeletal remains. In 1971, AIM disrupted archaeological excavations at Welch, Minnesota. This is one example of the ways that Pan-Indian political groups organized to try to stop or at least slow down the excavation of sacred sites and cemeteries. Such Pan-Indian groups also drew attention to the treatment of American Indian human remains and other sensitive material by museums through such means as the occupation of the Southwest Museum in Los Angeles in 1971. As they carried out these demonstrations, Indian groups also began to make known their desire for the repatriation of human remains and certain special cultural objects.

In the late 1960s and early '70s, Native groups such as the Onondagas began movements to retrieve cultural items from museums. Shown here are members of the tribe in 1970, picketing in front of the capitol building in Albany, New York, to demand that the New York State museum return several wampum belts, which Iroquoian people use in a number of sacred rituals.

In the 1970s, American Indian newspapers carried articles that outlined the general attitudes of these new Indian political groups. Prior to this time, any articles that were printed usually provided only general information about archaeological excavations or scientific theories about the peopling of North America. During the early 1970s, however, the orientation of news articles began to change. Rather than merely reporting on events, journalists tried to influence the ways in which the situation was presented. Newspapers printed articles that detailed the scientific excavation of skeletal material, as well as articles that called for anthropologists to stop practicing what some Indians thought was the exploitation of their culture. These articles were aimed at trying to influence American Indian readers about the practice of archaeology and anthropology.

In the early 1980s, important breakthroughs were made in relations between American Indian groups and the public and private sectors through the concerted efforts of individuals from tribes and museums. Museums returned certain objects of importance to American Indians, which helped clarify and confirm the value of such items to the continuing health of tribal culture. However, it was the development and passage of the National Museum of the American Indian Act (NMAIA) in 1989 and the Native American Graves Protection and Repatriation Act (NAGPRA) in 1990 that changed the underlying structures upon which the relationships between archaeologists and American Indians were based. Although scientists argued that the laws jeopardized their research, American Indians believed that science could no longer operate within the cultural and social vacuum it had operated under since Thomas Jefferson's investigations of the burial mounds in the 1780s.

Repatriation, in its basic sense, is the act of returning something to its native country. After wars, prisoners are "repatriated" to their home countries, usually with great fanfare. American Indian actions in the 1970s and 1980s were aimed at drawing attention to the fact that, in their belief, many important cultural items were—and still are—being held prisoner in foreign museums and that they need to be returned to their proper home.

3

Repatriation Legislation

It was only when Native people . . . rose to stop the racist practice
of the robbery and study of our graves was the "loss" to science
loudly and arrogantly lamented. Amid great gnashing of teeth,
the rush was on to study, document, analyze, and further
desecrate our relatives before the precious "scientific and
cultural materials" could be "destroyed" through reburial.[2]
—Jesse Taken Alive, chairman of the Standing Rock Sioux Tribe

BACKGROUND TO REPATRIATION

American Indian concerns relating to human remains are generally united in view in that most Native Americans do not wish Indian graves to be excavated in the first place. However, in situations where human remains have been excavated already, most tribes desire the human remains to be returned to the tribe of origin.

During the 1970s, various federal agencies had "in-house" policies affecting human remains. Within the Department of the Interior, the Interagency Archaeological Services maintained a "Policy for the Disposition of Human Remains" that served as a model for most other federal agencies involved with archaeological material. This policy called for the reburial of materials (after study) only when direct kinship or ethnic affinity to an individual could be demonstrated. Any human remains that could not be connected to particular families were to be maintained in repositories as federal property.

In 1978, Congress passed the American Indian Religious Freedom Act, legislation that required federal agencies to examine the ways their policies might impact the religious freedom of American Indians. One of the issues identified by American Indian groups was the status of human remains encountered in archaeological excavations and maintained in museum and institutional collections across the United States.

American Indian groups continued to push for the return of skeletal remains and to draw attention to the perceived inconsistency in the scientific study of American Indian human remains and the reburial of non-Indian remains encountered in projects. In response to this concern, twenty-three people participated in a conference on reburial issues at the Newberry Library's Darcy McNickle Center for the History of the American Indian in Chicago on June 14–15, 1985.

The invited participants represented a wide range of interest groups—academic and administrative archaeologists; American Indian spiritual, tribal, and political leaders; physical and cultural anthropologists; lawyers; museum administrators; and historians. Discussions centered around five major topics: 1) the reasons that American Indian tribes insisted upon reburial; 2) the reasons why scientists objected to reburial; 3) the reasons why scientists studied human skeletal populations; 4) exploration of possible resolutions to the perceived conflict; and 5) what should be taken as the next step.

The report of the meeting, in general, only restated what had been said before about the importance of respecting human remains: the need for public education; the need to protect human remains: from vandalism, looting, and desecration; and the hope for cooperation between anthropologists and American Indians. Additionally, it called for possible changes to existing federal laws, the introduction of new federal laws and regulations where appropriate, model state-level legislation regarding the return and reburial of American Indian human remains, and the matter of deaccession (sale or disposal) of the remains from museum collections.

The following year, on April 24, 1986, the Society for American Archaeology, the professional association organized to represent the wishes and views of American archaeologists, convened a special meeting on the treatment of human remains in New Orleans, Louisiana. This session's goal was to develop and refine a series of principles for ethical and socially responsible actions in situations that involved the excavation, analysis, curation, and ultimate disposition of human remains by archaeologists. This meeting resulted in the issuance of a "Statement Concerning the Treatment of Human Remains" in May 1986, which seemed to inflame the situation rather than ease the tension.

The document called for the concerns of different cultures to be channeled through designated representatives and leaders rather than expressed directly by concerned individuals themselves. It began from the position that all human remains should receive appropriate scientific study regardless of the situation, and was opposed to universal or indiscriminate reburial of human remains. It also came out against any potential federal legislation that would seek to impose a uniform standard for determining the disposition of all human remains.

Five months after the 1986 SAA meetings in New Orleans, the National Congress of American Indians adopted two resolutions that dealt with the treatment of any and all human remains exhumed by archaeologists. The first resolution condemned the U.S. Department of the Interior's policy regarding the disposition of human remains and recommended that the policy be tested in court. The second resolution was written in support of the efforts of Native governments and organizations to reclaim and protect their national treasures and cultural patrimony.

In April 1987, the Society of Professional Archaeologists proposed a reburial policy that dealt with ethical and legal considerations in the treatment of human remains that had at least fifty years of elapsed time following their interment. The policy called for exhumation when relocation or protection was not feasible and declared that the deliberate excavation of human remains for research or training purposes should not be condoned unless the remains are in danger. The policy called for the scientific community to balance the cultural and religious importance of the human remains to American Indian tribes with their significance in contemporary and predictable future research. Consultation with biological or culturally related groups of the deceased, including tribes currently or previously occupying the land in which the deceased lay, was also proposed. The policy suggested that no human remains or their related artifacts should be reburied until their research significance had been exhausted, although reinterment of human remains of "lesser significance" in accordance with state or local law and/or the wishes of biological or cultural descendants (or tribal groups who occupy or previously occupied the lands in which the deceased lay) should be allowed. Finally, the proposed policy called for the reinterment of human remains and associated grave artifacts that demonstrated cultural or religious significance of such magnitude that their analysis would impose an unconstitutional burden on the free exercise of religion by the deceased's descendants.

Another nationwide organization set up to represent anthropologists got involved in the debate shortly thereafter.

The American Anthropological Association set up a committee to study, report, and offer guidelines in regard to American Indian requests to rebury ancestral remains and associated grave goods held in museums, universities, and other depositories. The report by the so-called Reburial Commission provided an overview of the development of American anthropology and offered suggestions to guide activities at the local and national levels. The Reburial Commission proposed that more Indian people should be consulted and involved in the decision-making process, and suggested more networking between the Indian and anthropological communities. The commission's report also called for anthropologists to better educate tribal members about the historical usefulness of archaeology and biological anthropology; encouraged social science training for Native Americans; suggested the continued development of tribal and intertribal museums and cultural centers; and called for the production of timely reports and films on archaeological work that would be interesting to nonspecialists. In closing, the report stated that the controversy over human remains is not a simple issue of human rights or respect for the dead. "Human rights" does play a role in this controversy, however. American Indian religious practices and beliefs concerning human remains vary from tribal group to tribal group, but they generally believe that burial sites are spiritually important, the same way as some U.S. citizens think of cemeteries as being special and important. But, for a long time, American Indian human remains were not given the same treatment and respect as the skeletons of non-Indians.

In Iowa in 1971, a highway construction crew uncovered the bones of twenty-seven people. All of these people had been buried in a cemetery more than one hundred years prior to the discovery. Based on the materials in the graves, scientists determined one of the skeletons belonged to a young Indian woman and the other twenty-six were non-Indians. The remains of the non-Indians were reburied in a local cemetery, but the bones of the Indian woman were sent to a museum in Iowa City for storage.

Maria Pearson, a local American Indian woman, protested to the Office of the State Archaeologist about the unfair double standard applied to the Indian woman's skeleton. As a result of this protest, in 1981, Iowa became the first state to pass a reburial act to reinter American Indian human remains.

The Iowa law was one of the first laws that recognized the differential treatment afforded Indian skeletons and non-Indian ones. If you check into the laws of the state where you live, you probably will find that disturbing a grave or cemetery is against the law; but for a long time people could dig up American Indian graves without fear of being put in jail. In Texas, it is legal for landowners to dig up an "unmarked Indian burial"—one that is not in a marked cemetery or does not have a headstone—as long as it is on their land.

Anthropologists might view human skeletal material as important to science, but American Indian concerns about human remains extend beyond the physical bones themselves. The bones represent living people, not just pieces of calcium. The Navajos, for example, have a ceremony in which the sole purpose is to relieve what is called "ghost-sickness"—an illness caused by contact with spirits, ghosts, or places where ghosts are thought to reside. The importance of protecting the human remains of a culture from outsiders seems obvious, especially if tribal groups go to such extremes to protect themselves from the spirits associated with the remains.

Archaeologist Larry Zimmerman talks about the importance some tribal people place on skeletons. He quotes Lakota holy man Vernal Cross as saying he wanted to be cremated when he died so that ". . . maybe then I will be free of the white man." Mr. Cross' decision to be cremated was especially strong since this was not a traditional way of "burial" among the Lakota tribal group. Mr. Cross felt being cremated was the only way to keep from ending up in cardboard boxes, paper sacks, or plastic bags.³

SPEAKING OUT IN SUPPORT OF REPATRIATION

American Indian groups have been concerned about human remains in museum and archaeological collections for a long time. American Indian intertribal groups, such as American Indians Against Desecration and the American Indian Movement, became involved in trying to find ways to ensure that American Indian skeletons are returned to tribes and families. During hearings on the American Indian Religious Freedom Act of 1978, held across the United States, elected and traditional leaders of numerous tribes spoke out against the disturbance of Indian graves and cemeteries. They also spoke of their desires to have Indian skeletons reburied as close as possible to the places where they had been dug up.

Other organizations worked to have human remains removed from museums. In Kansas, for example, the Pawnee tribe worked to get a tourist attraction that exhibited Indian skeletons closed and the skeletons reburied; in Nebraska, they worked with other legislators to get a law passed that required the reburial of Indian skeletons. Such actions by tribal groups and groups of members of different tribes to get American Indian skeletal material reburied made it easier for nationwide legislation to be proposed and passed.

The National Museum of the American Indian Act and Its Amendment

With the passage of the National Museum of the American Indian Act (NMAIA) in 1989, Congress established the new National Museum of the American Indian and, at the same time, it required the Smithsonian Institution to inventory, document, and, if requested, repatriate culturally affiliated human remains and funerary objects to federally recognized Native groups. In 1996, the NMAIA was amended to add new categories of objects that would be subject to repatriation. It also established deadlines for the Smithsonian to distribute object summaries and inventories of its collections to tribes.

What Items Are Covered and Why?

Categories of materials that are eligible for return under the NMAIA include: 1) human remains of individuals whose identity is known; 2) culturally affiliated human remains; 3) associated and unassociated funerary objects; 4) sacred objects; and 5) objects of cultural patrimony. In addition, under longstanding museum policy, tribes may request the return of objects transferred to or acquired by the museum illegally or under circumstances that render the museum's claim to them invalid.

Culturally affiliated human remains are defined as human remains that share with a present-day Indian tribe a relationship that can be demonstrated based on a preponderance of available evidence. *Associated and unassociated funerary objects* are items that, as part of the death rites of a culture, are believed to have been intentionally placed with an individual of known affiliation at the time of death or later. Whether a funerary object is considered unassociated or associated depends only on whether or not the museum has the human remains with which it was originally interred: If the museum has the remains, funerary objects are associated, since there is a specific deceased person with whom to "associate" them. *Sacred objects* are specific ceremonial items that traditional Native American religious leaders need in order to allow present-day adherents to continue practicing their traditional religions. *Objects of cultural patrimony* are more difficult to define and often vary from tribe to tribe. In general, they are thought to be cultural items that were originally owned by the entire tribe, rather than by an individual, and which have an ongoing historical, traditional, or cultural importance to the Native group as a whole. Because the objects were tribally owned rather than individually owned, they cannot have been alienated, appropriated, or conveyed by any individual at the time they were acquired.

Native sacred objects are defined as items that spiritual leaders must have in order to carry out religious ceremonies. Shown here is a sacred Luiseno gourd rattle, which is decorated with sea turtles and used by California's Cahuilla tribe in religious ceremonies.

Examples of items of cultural patrimony for U.S. citizens might include the original Bill of Rights, the Liberty Bell, and the Statue of Liberty.

The Smithsonian was required to consider repatriation of Native American human remains and certain cultural objects to lineal descendants of named individuals, federally recognized Native American tribes, federally recognized Native Alaskan villages, and Native Hawaiian organizations named in the NMAIA. Requests from state-recognized Native American tribes are reviewed by the museum on a case-by-case basis.

The NMAIA also required the Smithsonian to establish a special committee to monitor and review the process of inventory, identification, and repatriation. This external review committee consists of seven individuals, four of whom must be

Native Americans. The review committee may, upon the request of any affected party, examine any findings relating to the origin or the return of human remains and cultural objects. The committee also assists the secretary of the Smithsonian in resolving disputes that may arise between groups or between a group and the Institution in regard to the disposition of collections.

On March 4, 1991, the National Museum of the American Indian adopted a new policy on the repatriation of Native American human remains and cultural materials. It committed the museum to dispose of human remains, funerary objects, and objects transferred or acquired illegally or under circumstances that render the museum's claim to them invalid or questionable. The policy set forth a number of principles regarding the handling and treatment of objects. Basically, the goals of the policy are oriented toward supporting the continuation of ceremonial and ritual life among Native Americans, toward supporting Native Americans who wish to study their own traditions, and toward forging a consensus between the museum and Native American communities.

The Native American Graves Protection and Repatriation Act

The Native American Graves Protection and Repatriation Act (NAGPRA) affirms the rights of lineal descendants, Indian tribes, and Native Hawaiian organizations to custody of Native American human remains, funerary objects, sacred items, and objects of cultural patrimony held in federal museums or agencies, or in museums that receive federal funds. Signed into law by President George H.W. Bush in November 1990, NAGPRA places the responsibility for compliance upon federal agencies and museums that receive federal funds. It required all federal departments, agencies, or instrumentalities of the United States (except for the Smithsonian Institution) to complete summaries and inventories of Native American materials in their control (including those held by nongovernmental repositories). The affected organizations were also ordered to ensure compliance regarding inadvertent discoveries and intentional excavations of human remains conducted as part of activities on federal or tribal lands.

Museums as defined in NAGPRA are more than just places that house artifacts and collections. Under NAGPRA, museums include any institution or state or local government agency (including any institution of higher learning) that has possession of, or control over, items covered under the act and that receives federal funds. The two important terms—*possession*, meaning the physical custody of objects with sufficient legal interest to lawfully treat them as part of the museum's collection, and *control*, having a sufficient legal interest in objects to lawfully permit the museum to treat the objects as part of its collection, whether or not the objects are in the physical custody of the museum—were also defined. Generally, a museum that has loaned objects to any entity (individual, museum, or federal agency) is considered to retain control of those items, although the objects may not be in the physical custody of the museum. Objects in the museum's collection that have been received on loan from another individual, museum, or federal agency are considered under the control of the loaning museum.

NAGPRA also provided an expanded definition of the phrase "receives federal funds." As defined in the act, a museum that receives funds from a federal agency through any grant, loan, contract (other than a procurement contract), or arrangement by which a federal agency makes or made available funds to a museum is included. If a larger entity of which the museum is a part receives federal funds (that is, a university museum where the university receives federal funds), then the museum must comply with NAGPRA regulations. NAGPRA also applies to certified local governments and tribal museums if they receive federal funds through any grant, loan, or contract. The act does not apply to private individuals and museums that do not receive federal funds and that are not part of a larger entity that does receive federal funds.

The statute lays out a mechanism for federal land managers, museums, and agency officials to consult with lineal descendants and tribal groups and to reach a determination regarding the proper disposition of objects covered under the act that might be excavated or discovered on federal or tribal lands. The processes for dealing with excavations or discoveries on federal or tribal lands are different from those for dealing with the disposition of objects within museum or federal agency collections.

Who Has the Right to Claim Materials Covered under These Laws?

According to NMAIA and NAGPRA, there are various categories of people who have the right to make a claim for the items covered under either law. The people who can make a claim vary depending upon the item under consideration.

For human remains, lineal descendants (those who can demonstrate direct ancestry to a named individual) have the first right to reclaim skeletal material. If there are no lineal descendants, or if the identity of the individual skeleton is unknown, then the tribe of the individual can request a return. If the tribe is not known, then the tribe on whose land the set of human remains was found can request the return of the material. Finally, if the remains were not found on tribal land, then the tribe on whose aboriginal territory the remains were found can request a return.

In the case of unassociated grave goods, the priority of claimants is similar, going through the tribe that is likely to have produced the items, the tribal group on whose land the materials were found, and then the tribal group on whose aboriginal territory the materials were found.

Finally, in the case of sacred items and objects of cultural patrimony, only the tribe that claims the artifacts can make a request. Since by their very nature such artifacts cannot be owned by individuals, only entire tribes are allowed to make requests for returns.

Native American groups hailed the passage of NAGPRA as an opportunity to right centuries-old wrongs perpetrated against American Indian graves. In a symposium sponsored by the *Arizona State Law Journal,* many authors discussed the law as it impacted various institutions that dealt with Native American human remains and cultural material.

While the passage of NAGPRA gave American Indians some of the tools necessary to implement the changes they had demanded in the 1970s, some American Indians complained that scientists were using the inventories and summaries required of museums as a means of obtaining additional scientific data under the guise of complying with the new law. Though the law does not authorize the initiation of new scientific studies, it does not preclude it when the museum deems such research necessary for determining the cultural affiliation of a set of human remains or when the materials are indispensable for completion of a specific scientific study, the outcome of which would be of major benefit to the United States.

Many American Indian groups question why the graves protection portion of NAGPRA was not applied to all lands within the United States, rather than just to federal or tribal lands, since the entire continent was at one time Indian land. The National Congress of American Indians, the oldest and largest national organization representing Native Americans, called for changes to NAGPRA to extend protection of funerary remains and objects on all lands within the exterior boundaries of the United States, wherever they may be situated. NAGPRA Review Committee Chairwoman Tessie Naranjo of Santa Clara Pueblo noted that the review committee itself experienced frustration over this issue. Although human remains may be protected under various state laws, federal intervention on private land is sometimes seen as a violation of the "takings clause" of the Constitution if the landowner is somehow denied access or free use of his or her property without adequate compensation.

Another point of concern to American Indians is in relation to Native American human remains and funerary objects whose cultural affiliation has not been established. Even the NAGPRA Review Committee felt that this issue was a point of frustration. Dan Monroe, a member of the committee in 1996, noted in testimony that this is a major point of contention, especially in respect to the disposition of ancient Native American remains, which can seldom be associated with a specific tribe.

In 1998, the NAGPRA Review Committee issued a set of Draft Principles of Agreement Regarding the Disposition of Culturally Unidentifiable Human Remains. This document presented guidelines for the ultimate disposition of these types of remains. Although no specific remedies are defined for every case, the principles do offer suggestions for disposition in cases where the human remains are associated with a nonfederally recognized tribe. They also suggest regional consultations where such approaches would prove beneficial and for situations where the human remains represent a population for which there are no present-day cultural survivors.

The passage of the National Museum of the American Indian Act and the Native American Graves Protection and Repatriation Act caused the disciplines of archaeology and biological anthropology to react strongly, perhaps more strongly than necessary. The importance of human remains in the study of past diets, lifeways, and cultures has been recognized by various authors, but archaeologists nonetheless failed to make clear the objectives of hoping to retain control over human remains and cultural objects discovered during excavations.

The impact of the law's requirements was immediately felt by those museums that were required to prepare inventories of the human remains and associated grave goods, sacred items, and objects of cultural patrimony within their collections. The inventories were then forwarded to American Indian groups that were often forced to wade through lengthy computer printouts in an effort to pinpoint those items in which they had an interest. The sudden influx of such lists strained tribal staffs, whose organizations were often already underfunded, and forced some tribes to either curtail aspects of their cultural resource programs or to try to come to grips with the mountain of data they didn't know what to do with.

Archaeologists and organizations were quick to recognize the problems involved in consultation and repatriation of material recovered or donated before the current legislative controls, but legal analyses of NAGPRA pointed out that archaeologists were not entitled to own the materials that the tribes were requesting. Control of such objects covered under the law was vested in the tribes or in particular members of the tribes.

Whereas museum officials and curators might have been concerned about the loss of items from their collections, archaeologists appeared to be more worried about the loss of the freedom to pursue "science" and the academic quest for answers to questions that may not be of concern to many American Indians. Anthropologists soon entered into the legal arena in a fight to retain their right to attempt to answer questions that influence the worldwide knowledge base.

The Kennewick Controversy

In 1996, when a nearly complete set of human remains was discovered on the shore of the Columbia River in Washington State by a couple of college students, no one could foresee that the result would eventually be a court challenge of many of the major tenets of NAGPRA. The area containing the human remains was originally treated as a crime scene by Dr. James Chatters, the Benton County coroner and an archaeologist, because that is the way most discoveries of human remains are

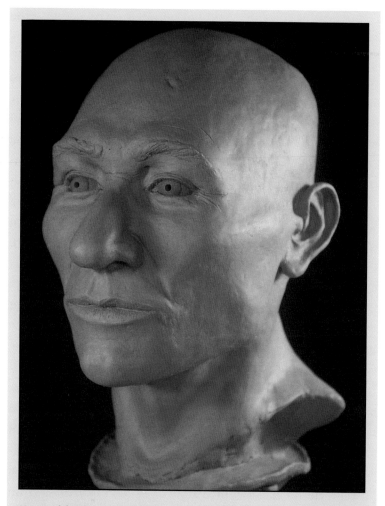

Kennewick Man, whose head is portrayed here in a clay model, was discovered by two college students on the shore of the Columbia River in central Washington State in 1996. After radiocarbon tests were conducted on a portion of his bone, it was determined by scientists that he was approximately 9,200 years old. In February 2004, it was ruled by the United States Court of Appeals for the Ninth Circuit that there is no direct evidence that can link him with any tribe, thus his remains are currently being housed at the Burke Museum in Seattle, Washington.

initially handled. After a flaked stone projectile point was discovered embedded in the pelvis of the skeleton, Chatters sent off a portion of bone to a radiocarbon laboratory. When the results came back indicating that the remains were approximately 9,200 years old, NAGPRA went into action.

The human remains were treated as an "inadvertent discovery" under NAGPRA, and the U.S. Army Corps of Engineers (which controlled the federal land upon which the remains were found) determined to repatriate the remains to the Umatilla tribe. However, shortly before the remains were to be returned, eight anthropologists filed suit in district court to block the repatriation. One of those anthropologists, Rob Bonnichsen, expressed the beliefs of the group: "There's a whole book of information [in Kennewick Man's bones]. To put him back in the ground is like burning a rare book so we'll learn nothing. . . . It seems to be the case there is a major effort to block scientific inquiry into the study of American origins."[4]

From the beginning, the remains intrigued scientists, but American Indians were not willing to allow anthropologists to keep them for further study. To representatives of the Umatilla, it did not matter how old the remains were—the tribe still considered the individual an American Indian. Armand Minthorn, a member of the Confederated Tribes of the Umatilla Indians—one of the tribes claiming the set of human remains—talked about the fact that tribes do not feel that scientists are the only ones who can outline the history of tribal groups. He noted how, in many tribes, history is passed on through elders and through religious practices, and they do not rely upon science to tell their members about their past.

Thus, the problem at the outset was not a question of science versus religion, as some of the popular press reported, but more a conflict between American Indian philosophy and the unilateral application of American science. Not even all U.S. anthropologists agreed in their philosophy. Articles and letters in professional journals discussed the political and academic implications of Kennewick, especially in relation to the scientific and social definitions of "race."

The court case involving the scientists and the U.S.

Department of the Interior over the disposition of the human remains continued from October 1996 until magistrate John Jelderks reached a decision in August 2002. The lawsuit was put on hold for a while, so that the Department of the Interior could perform tests on the skeleton in an attempt to better determine the "cultural affiliation" of the human remains. One of these studies subjected the bones to statistical analyses of skeletal measurements in an attempt to find any morphological relationships between the skeleton and other world populations.

Osteological analyses (the study of bones) on the Kennewick Man, which was performed by Joseph Powell and Jerome Rose of the Department of the Interior's scientific team, raised some interesting paradoxes. Statistical tests conducted on the skull led them to conclude that the Kennewick skeleton could be excluded on the basis of dental and cranial morphology from the population of recent American Indians. More importantly, the scientists reached a conclusion that the skeleton can be excluded (on the basis of typicality probabilities) from *all* late Holocene (recent) human groups. Yet, their research also pointed out that the Kennewick cranium is morphologically similar to later populations from the northern Great Basin region and to large populations in the Eastern Woodlands, suggesting that the human populations of North America that followed the Paleoindian time period (c. 13000–8000 B.C.) *may* have derived some of their morphological characteristics from the population of which the Kennewick individual was a member.

With the publication of the results of these analyses on the skeletal material, it became obvious that science was facing the possibility of losing an example of one of the "founder populations" of North America. The fact that the skeleton was not related to any recent human group, especially any American Indian group, made it more difficult to justify repatriating it to any particular Indian tribe and easier to argue in favor of continued study. The principal issue raised throughout the conflict was the legal question of whether the Native American Graves Protection and Repatriation Act should apply to materials of antiquity.

If truly ancient remains such as those in the Kennewick case are excluded from protection or disposition under NAGPRA, a court would need to provide guidance as to what age categorizes human remains as "ancient," as well as whether science or tribal oral history should be used to define that threshold. The NAGPRA Review Committee has partially addressed this issue, but it has yet to be resolved. Additionally, the court decision might also affect the scientific exception clause of NAGPRA, which allows for the scientific study of materials when the results of that research are deemed to be of potentially major benefit to the U.S. government. The study of human remains of such antiquity will likely be deemed to be of benefit to the United States, especially in relation to information that might be obtained regarding early peoples of the New World, but, since NAGPRA is silent on this issue in regard to inadvertent discoveries, the court decision would likely set a precedent regarding legislative intent.

On February 4, 2004, the United States Court of Appeals for the Ninth Circuit in Washington State finally ruled on the Kennewick case. It found that NAGPRA's grave protection laws do not apply to the Kennewick remains because there is no direct evidence that can link the remains with any modern existing tribe. The Umatilla, Colville, and Nez Perce tribes, who have been seeking to repatriate the remains, were greatly upset by the decision. The Colville Tribe's attorney, Rob Roy Smith, said the ruling was "a great injustice" and stated: "The 9th Circuit turned the statute [NAGPRA] on its head. . . . The law Congress passed gives tribes the right to prevent the study of remains. What the 9th Circuit seems to have done is to require the tribes to prove the remains are Native American before the statute applies."[5]

Summary

The two major repatriation laws—the National Museum of the American Indian Act and the Native American Graves Protection and Repatriation Act—both set the stage for American Indian groups to regain human remains and certain classes of cultural items that had somehow found their way into museums across the country. The two laws set up various rankings of priority that gave groups of Indians the right to request these human remains and artifacts, provided that they could demonstrate the proper relationship to the items.

Museums were tasked with providing listings of the materials in their collections that were covered by the laws, and tribes were left with the job of trying to determine whether the items on lists that the museums provided related to them. Both groups were forced to work together to find ways to meet their mutual responsibilities under the laws.

The two repatriation laws are not perfect, and both Indians and non-Indians alike have recognized some of the problems that the two laws do not address, or areas where the laws do not go far enough to protect American Indian human remains. At least, however, the laws were written with the purpose of trying to get American Indian human remains out of museums and back to the tribes where they belong.

4

Repatriation and Anthropology

We want the public and scientists to understand that we do not reject science. In fact, we have anthropologists and other scientists on staff, and we use science every day to help in protecting our people and the land. However, we do reject the notion that science is the answer to everything and therefore it should take precedence over the religious rights and beliefs of American citizens.[6]
—Don Sampson, former Board of Trustees chairman for the Confederated Tribes of the Umatilla Indian Reservation

As we discussed in chapter 2, *anthropology* in its broadest sense is the comprehensive study of humankind. It tries to understand cultures by comparing human groups and analyzing the ways in which they are different and similar from each other. Also, as discussed earlier, repatriation means "returning something to the country to which it belongs." Two branches of anthropology are involved in working with American Indian human remains and cultural items—archaeology and biological anthropology—and each is affected by repatriation differently.

WHAT IS ARCHAEOLOGY?

For many people, mention of the word *archaeology* conjures up images of Indiana Jones running through a South American temple carrying a golden idol while dodging poison darts, or Lara Croft raiding tombs in search of sacred objects to save the world. Other people have a better idea of what archaeology is and can link it to the study of Egyptian mummies or ancient Greek and Roman civilizations. Some people are completely off the mark and think archaeology deals with dinosaurs! Archaeology does not involve golden idols and tomb robbing, and definitely not dinosaurs!

Archaeology is the study of the human past through its material remains, and *archaeologists* are the people who use sites to learn about people of the past in order to better understand the people of today. Archaeology is considered a "social science" because it uses the scientific method to try to gain knowledge about the social world (human world) in the same way that other scientists try to gain information about the natural world. Scientists use observation, hypothesis formulation, experimentation, observation, hypothesis refinement, more observation, and so on, to try to gain as much information as possible to explain how things "work."

What Use Are American Indian Materials to Archaeologists?

Archaeology uses American Indian materials to help understand the ways that people adapt to climate and changing areas through culture, technology, and other aspects. The earliest inhabitants of the North American continent are called "Paleoindians," and came into North America between ten thousand and perhaps twenty thousand years ago. By studying the particular styles of projectile points (spear points) that Paleoindians made of flint and chert, we can understand how they were able to use natural resources to hunt large mammoths and bison. By studying the places where they lived and hunted, we can learn about how they knew their territories. By studying the animals they killed, we can understand how the climate has changed since they lived there. And, by looking at the human skeletons of the people who were alive at that time, we can learn about how people in North America themselves have changed over the last ten thousand to twenty thousand years.

Archaeologists are interested in the material remains (*artifacts*) that are used, lost, and discarded by humans throughout time. These artifacts can give us glimpses into the world of the people of the past in much the same way that looking at your room can give someone else clues about the type of person you might be.

But artifacts by themselves have very little meaning. A beautiful arrowhead without *context* (the relationship between one artifact and the other artifacts or cultural deposits in a site or area) is nothing more than a pretty thing. To archaeologists, the context is what helps explain the sites and the artifacts within it. For example, an arrowhead taken from a site and shown to an archaeologist can only give information about the stone that the arrowhead is made from and perhaps (if the archaeologist can *really* trust the person who brought in the arrowhead) that the arrowhead comes from a certain site. However, if the same person leaves the arrowhead in place and takes an archaeologist to the site, then the archaeologist can use the relationships between the arrowhead and other artifacts at the site to construct a better picture of the different events that might have happened at the place. Science and archaeology gain more information about the human past by looking at and recording artifacts left at a site than they can by looking at artifacts taken out of context.

Cahokia Mounds, which are located near Collinsville, Illinois, were the site of the largest city in North America during the twelfth to fourteenth centuries A.D. Much like the Spiro Mounds in Oklahoma, Cahokia was pilfered by treasure-seekers and archaeologists, but today it is protected by the Illinois Historic Preservation Agency.

Because it is the relationships between artifacts that are most important, archaeologists also try to educate people about the damage done to our understanding of the past when unqualified people disturb archaeological sites. This disturbance may be done accidentally through activities such as farming, construction, or even motorcycle riding. Almost any activity done in areas where people once lived can damage archaeological sites. Other people purposefully disturb archaeological sites in order to find the cultural material that might be present.

In the 1930s, for example, people dug into and even used dynamite to destroy a large burial mound in eastern Oklahoma to get the artifacts that had been buried with the Indians. The Spiro Mounds were nearly destroyed then, and many of the artifacts collected were taken to museums in New York, Chicago, and even places as far away as Germany and Japan. It was because of these unscientific and destructive practices that the State of Oklahoma developed laws to try to protect the archaeological materials for all the people of Oklahoma to be able to see and appreciate. This was one of the first sets of laws in the United States designed to protect cultural resources. Today, people caught excavating or destroying archaeological sites on federally owned or controlled lands without a special permit are subject to a monetary fine and perhaps a prison sentence as well.

There are numerous components of Indian history in North America that interest archaeologists, and each individual archaeologist has questions that he or she would like to answer. Some archaeologists are interested in the ways that the early people who came to North America adapted to the different climates, animals, and unknown landscapes they encountered. Some are interested in how the development of farming and such crops as corn changed the ways American Indian populations lived. Others are interested in how the use of corn as food impacted the health of the American Indian populations, because the sugar in the corn led to increased cavities in the teeth among people who ate large quantities of it.

So, clearly, archaeology uses the material remains from people of the past in order to better understand the various ways that humans have found to survive and flourish. Without archaeology, we would perhaps only be able to understand human history five thousand years back in time, because the invention of writing, the basis for "history," has been around only that long. For some groups, such as the American Indians, writing has only been around for one hundred or two hundred years, and, for others, it became available only very recently. Archaeology offers a way of "digging into the past" for those areas where writing has not long existed, but it does lead to a different understanding and interpretation of the past.

What Use Is Archaeology to American Indians?

This has been a major question that both American Indian groups and archaeologists have been trying to answer. At first, archaeology does not seem suited to answering questions that American Indians might want answered, but that is only on the surface.

Archaeology has the opportunity, as noted before, to help tribes gain an understanding of the long-term use of the area where they currently live. The archaeological record—the cultural and natural materials that are found at archaeological sites—provides a myriad of information about the cultures that lived in the site area. Archaeologists can look at the complex of materials they find and gain insights into the ways the cultures adapted to or coped with their environment.

During the Archaic period (c. 4000–250 B.C.) in the southern Great Plains, for example, the archaeological record is relatively bleak. Few sites are known for a span of time that exceeds six thousand years. At one time, it appeared that people had abandoned much of the area because the hot and dry weather conditions made it difficult to survive. Archaeologists have found, however, that people continued to occupy the area but relied more on plant resources to fulfill their dietary needs and relied less on large animals like bison. The archaeological record left behind by the people on the southern Great Plains during the Archaic period indicates a group of people who chose to adapt to a changing environment rather than leave.

Another use tribes may have for archaeology is the role the archaeologist can play as an expert witness in court cases regarding lands that Indians once occupied or lands that are the subject of other legal proceedings. For example, about five hundred years ago, a group of people living in the southern Great Plains in an area within the present-day states of Kansas and Oklahoma survived by growing corn and hunting buffalo. These people lived in villages; in houses constructed in a specific manner. And they made easily recognized pottery and arrowheads. When Spanish explorer Francisco Vásquez de Coronado encountered and wrote about them in 1541, he called them the "Quivira." Archaeologists now think that the people Coronado encountered were members of a Wichita group called the Tawakoni, and found that, in 1609, they had moved to the Red River, 120 miles farther south. By working on the sites left by the Quivirans, as well as sites that are older than those mentioned by Coronado, archaeologists provide scientific information that can provide more depth to the unwritten histories of tribal groups in North America. These investigations also provide information that allows tribes to demonstrate more fully which lands they occupied at the time of historic contact with Europeans, as well as the lands on which they lived before Europeans entered the continent.

It should be emphasized, however, that archaeologists are not the only ones who are able to provide information to help extend a tribe's history back into time. American Indians are curious about their history and they do not believe that all scientific and social studies are without value. They are also aware that anthropologists, archaeologists, and historians have filled gaps in tribal history. The conflict arises when archaeologists assume that only they are the caretakers and owners of the past and do not respect the idea that Indians have oral histories that are as meaningful to tribal people as science is to the archaeologist. Many tribal members maintain oral histories that tell of how a tribe has existed through time and how the tribe developed. Armand Minthorn succinctly states the view held by many American Indians:

> Some scientists say that if this individual is not studied further, we, as Indians, will be destroying evidence of our own history. We already know our history. It is passed on to us through our elders and through our religious practices.
>
> Scientists have dug up and studied American Indians for decades. We view this practice as desecration of the body and

a violation of our most deeply held religious beliefs. Our beliefs and policies also tell us this individual must be reburied as soon as possible.[7]

Archaeology does not presume to be the only way to provide additional time-depth to tribal histories, but it offers a more scientific way of viewing the material of the past.

WHAT IS BIOLOGICAL ANTHROPOLOGY?

In addition to archaeologists, *biological anthropologists* often study American Indian skeletal remains. At the beginning of chapter 2, a brief description of biological anthropology and the focus of its studies were given, but now a more detailed examination of the benefits that scientists obtain from studying American Indian skeletal material will be presented.

What Use Are American Indian Materials to Biological Anthropologists?

In the past, anthropologists would often take American Indian remains from marked cemeteries and even relatively fresh graves in order to study the skeletal structures. Most of these activities were done in small settlements and under cover of darkness, but not all such activity was carried out that way. In 1898, the American Museum of Natural History in New York performed a fake funeral to hide the fact it had kept the body of an Inuit man who had died while visiting the city rather than burying the body or returning it to the man's son. The scientists apparently thought the chance to study an Inuit's bones was worth deceiving the man's child. Today, it is unlikely that there is a single scientist who would stoop to such tactics to obtain study materials.

As you read through the history of anthropology's fascination with American Indians, it sometimes seems "macabre" or "weird." It seems strange to think that anyone would want to steal the bones of a known person without asking the consent of the next of kin, but anthropologists at one time did in the name of scientific research. Some of them justified such actions based on the idea that the Indians were vanishing and that "pure" Indians would be impossible to find in the future.

Why did anthropologists wish to study American Indian human remains? In a sometimes grisly history, anthropologists were intrigued by the people who had occupied this continent prior to European conquest. The Mound Builder controversy discussed in chapter 2 led some anthropologists to dig up American Indian graves in order to see whether the skulls of the existing Indians were similar to the skulls of the Mound Builder. They thought that, if the skulls looked similar, it might prove whether the Indians were the descendants of the Mound Builders or whether the Mound Builders were indeed a separate race. There were other researchers who thought that American Indians were "primitive" (comparing Indian cultures to European cultures) because their brains were smaller than those of the Europeans, rather than viewing Indian cultures as a product of their environment.

The Native American Graves Protection and Repatriation Act falls heavily on those individuals who analyze and interpret the human remains subject to repatriation, as well as on those who initially encounter those remains. Biological anthropologists and osteologists often discuss the types of information that can be obtained by studying human remains. These articles are often construed by American Indians to be nothing more than a justification for the continued study of human remains, but they nonetheless offer an attempt to educate not only American Indians but also other anthropologists about the uses of osteological information concerning the lifestyles of human beings.

Have you ever seen television specials that relate to forensics—the scientific study of the human body to determine the identity or the cause of death or trauma? Recently, forensics has been made popular by television shows, such as *CSI* and *CSI: Miami*, in which the investigators collect physical evidence at a crime scene or from a dead body to determine how a victim was killed. Biological anthropologists might be considered a similar sort of detective.

In a paper written in 1996, two biological anthropologists—Patricia M. Landau and D. Gentry Steele—gave nine reasons why anthropologists study human remains. They discussed how physical anthropologists seek to understand the biological history and origins of all humans in all geographical areas and the ways that each society's biological history is an integral part of the complete and continuing story of all humankind.

They discussed why the information they obtain from skeletal remains is unique, and why it can't be acquired from living peoples. Biological anthropology, according to Landau and Steele, provides direct information about all of the world's ancestors, and the information gathered during the analysis of human remains can provide data that can come from no other source—information that other disciplines, such as history or sociology, may be able to supplement but not replace.

Biological anthropologists are also interested in what they can learn about our ancestral origins from the study of human remains, especially in relation to specific studies such as the origins of the first inhabitants of North and South America. In an example they give, Landau and Steele discussed the way that biological anthropologists have used studies of human teeth to postulate that there have been at least three migrations of people into North America. Why is the number of migrations of people important? It probably has little bearing on most of our day-to-day living, but it helps anthropologists understand the various contributions that different cultural and physical groups have made to the population that is now recognized as American Indian.

Like the television detectives, biological anthropologists are able to gather information about the behavior of past peoples through the study of human remains. They are able to infer activities of past populations based on irregularities in skeletal

Biological anthropologists use DNA material from human remains to study the origins of various cultures. For instance, the study of Native American bloodlines can provide answers to American Indians' genetic heritage. However, the study of Native remains is controversial because many American Indian groups believe that human skeletal remains should be reburied.

and dental morphology. Muscle attachments on specific areas of the bone increase with an increase in muscle size, thereby offering glimpses into the lifestyle of populations. Another study showed that differential tooth wear among women in a certain culture was related to their role in using their teeth to soften animal skins. In essence, biological anthropology helps paint a picture of the daily life of past peoples.

How do anthropologists gather information from human remains? There are various means of acquiring information, including visual observation of anatomical characteristics such as broken and healed bones, tooth wear, suture closings, and so forth. Microscopic examination of skeletal material requires some alteration of the bones, sometimes involving taking thin slices of bone or teeth. Osteometric analyses require calipers and particular measurements but can help answer general questions such as ancestral/descendant relationships and the health and nutrition of the deceased, while also providing some indication of estimated stature of the individual.

Biological anthropologists often maintain that the repatriation of human skeletal material in museums would deprive them of the opportunity to restudy human remains. American Indians ask why such restudy is necessary. Landau and Steele explain that the testing, retesting, and expanding of interpretations that makes up the field of biological anthropology is often dependent on the restudy of the biological remains recovered from archaeological or burial sites. Technological advances, the development of new methods that include more sophisticated research designs, and the accompanying shifts in scientific perspectives are all reasons to restudy remains. Each of these also influences the development of new interests. For example, biological anthropological works of the 1930s were overwhelmingly descriptive in character; descriptive reports dominated the 1940s, but a slight rise in methods of identification of age, sex, and race was also evident. The 1950s saw continued interest in descriptive reports, but the decade also saw an increase in studies of growth, development, maturation, and ageing. Investigations in the 1960s looked at paleodemography (the geographic distribution of human populations in the past), growth, stature, and health status. The restudy of human remains allows anthropologists to reevaluate conclusions reached in earlier studies, to test new hypotheses and methods in the field in general, and to move forward in understanding past Native American populations, and, by extension, all humans past and present.

Biological anthropology, while it may be used to study individuals, is also concerned with gathering information on as many individuals as possible. Data from a single human being can give biological anthropologists information, but the study and compilation of information from large numbers of individuals allow anthropologists to generalize about other people in the same society. Without the examination of large numbers of specimens, biological anthropologists cannot be sure that their data are representative of the society as a whole and are not idiosyncratic characteristics of the few individuals studied. They also need to examine large numbers of individuals to determine the range of variation within a population.

Why do analyses take such a long time? Basic information about the minimum number of individuals represented by the material, including age and gender, are often determined during the initial analysis. Trauma, disease or other disorders, nutritional status, gross morphological characteristics, and other concerns are complex undertakings and require more specialized analyses, sometimes including chemical or other invasive techniques. Another important issue warranting the long-term study of human remains is the rarity of some sets of remains. The Paleoindian period is an example: The small number of individuals that have been found from approximately eleven thousand years ago and the poor preservation of the human remains make it difficult to obtain an adequate sample to provide reliable scientific information about the people who were the first inhabitants of the Western Hemisphere.

What Use Is Biological Anthropology to American Indians?

All the aforementioned points are basic reasons why biological anthropologists study human remains, but perhaps the most pointed question relating to the repatriation of American Indian human remains is: How does the study of human remains, particularly the study of Native American remains, benefit living people?

To demonstrate benefits, biological anthropologists point to the ways that the study of prehistoric and historic skeletal samples has aided our understanding of the patterns of early development of rheumatoid arthritis. This knowledge may be used in the future to aid in the treatment of living people suffering from the disease.

Some American Indians understand that it is quite possible that, at one time, the study of osteology did play a role in the advancement of medicine and proper diet and the prevention of bone disease, but they now argue that the sophistication of modern medicine makes it less likely that further excavation and examination of Native people is necessary, at least in regard to the three reasons mentioned. If, however, biological anthropology could provide usable information that would help alleviate medical problems, American Indians would likely support more biological anthropological study of American Indian remains.

Take diabetes, for example. Many American Indians suffer from the impacts of this disease, in which the pancreas does not produce or process insulin properly. Insulin is used to help the body break down sugar, starches, and other food into the energy needed for daily life. The cause of diabetes continues to be a mystery, although both genetics and environmental factors, such as obesity and lack of exercise, appear to play roles.

In the past, American Indians were able to eat large amounts of food on a seasonal basis and, naturally, gain weight, in a so-called "feast or famine" lifestyle. As food became less available, and as the people walked in search of other food, the exercise and decreased intake of food likely prevented diabetes from becoming a major problem in their lives. However, when American Indians began growing corn and settling in one place, they didn't exercise as much as they did in the past—they weren't walking as much, searching for food. This decrease in exercise, coupled with the increased intake of corn with its high sugar content, probably began to put a strain on the pancreas. Corn had another benefit—once dried, it could be stored for long periods of time. In this manner, it served as a "hedge" against lean harvest years. However, this hedge soon turned into a sure thing, and people began to follow diets high in carbohydrates and to exercise less and less. Eventually, the decrease in exercise and increase in carbohydrates led many Indians to contract diabetes.

And so, based on these facts, if anthropologists or archaeologists could help American Indians understand how their ancestors coped with environmental stress and the ways their ancestors' bodies were able to store fats and excess carbohydrates, perhaps the incidence of diabetes within American Indian populations would decline and American Indians would support continued research in the field.

One tribal group in Oklahoma has developed a relationship with a biological anthropologist to study human remains. The Wichita and Confederated Bands of Oklahoma has worked with a biological anthropologist to try to develop characteristics of precontact human skeletons that can be identified as "Wichita" so that, if skeletons with those characteristics are identified from archaeological sites later on, the tribe might be able to better prove its geographical range during precontact times. Additionally, the Caddo and Quapaw tribes of Oklahoma were involved in a program of osteological analysis whereby certain traits (including extra teeth, failure of teeth to develop, depressed occipital bones in the skull, and depressions on the bones of the shoulder blades) were examined in skeletons within archaeological collections in order to aid in determining cultural affiliation as required under NAGPRA.

The core of the conflict that exists between biological anthropologists and American Indians is largely the result of different worldviews. Many American Indians see the disturbance of burials as offensive to religious beliefs. Biological anthropologists have been cast as representing the source of evils associated with the desecration of the dead in their role as dispassionate scientists who have taken the "right" to excavate, study, and retain skeletal material in the name of science and education.

But the problem is not merely the scientists' perspectives but a more general one. It is part of a larger set of ideas that have developed over the nearly four hundred years of European occupation of North America based on different aspects of land ownership.

As the English and other European colonists settled in North America, they needed more and more land to grow crops to feed themselves. As the population in the east and the need for land grew, the United States entered into more and more treaties with Indian tribes for land. Tribes signed treaties to give up tracts of land in exchange for promises of protection, money, and other lands to the west. As a result, tribes were pushed farther away from the lands where they lived and where their dead were buried.

Eventually, large tracts of land were provided for the settlers and moved into private ownership. The idea of private ownership carried with it the idea that people who owned the land owned everything on their property, including American Indian graves and cultural material.

But the worldviews of the Americans and American Indians seemed to be at odds. Americans protected the graves of their dead and erected monuments to mark their final resting places but failed to extend the same level of consideration to the graves of American Indians. Perhaps the failure to consider the graves of American Indians as special is because they were not "marked" in the same ways as those of the Americans and other Europeans.

United States law also failed to protect the unmarked graves of American Indians. As noted in chapter 3, it wasn't until 1981 that Iowa gave equal treatment of human skeletal remains from

American Indians to those of non-American Indians. In some states only law officials or specially qualified individuals can excavate human burials, and then only with a special permit. Despite attempts to change Texas law in 2003, a landowner can still dig up unmarked human graves and "own" the skeletal remains without penalty.

And so, because of the various laws and the unequal ways American Indian and non-Indian skeletons and graves are viewed, is it any wonder that some of America's scientists still think it is OK to "own" American Indian skeletal remains? Many American scientists have realized that maintaining American Indian human remains in museums while reburying non-Indian human remains is wrong. Others, however, believe it is important to study the skeletal remains before returning them. A third group, however, believes it is important to maintain the human skeletal remains in scientific institutions for future generations.

American Indian groups believe it necessary for all American Indian human skeletal remains to be reburied. They argue that nothing can excuse the unequal treatment of American Indian and non-Indian skeletal remains. They argue that, until skeletal remains are treated equally, American Indians cannot be considered equal to the dominant society. They argue that human skeletons were humans and should be treated as such, not treated as objects for study like pots and arrowheads.

How Has NAGPRA Impacted Anthropology?

So far, NAGPRA has had only a minimal impact on archaeology and archaeological collections. As stated earlier, few archaeologists actually are involved with the materials that are covered by the repatriation aspects of NAGPRA or NMAIA. Biological anthropology, however, has been impacted by the repatriation clauses of NAGPRA.

Although some anthropologists feared that NAGPRA

would usher in the wholesale decimation of skeletal collections and would mean the end of biological anthropology, that has not been the case. Some archaeologists have found that NAG-PRA has actually contributed to biological anthropology and osteology in several different ways. First, because of the inventory requirements of the law, gaps in knowledge about specific time periods or geographical areas are being filled. Additionally, the inventory process is ensuring that the locations of skeletal remains are known and recorded, providing a database of skeletal locations and cultural affiliations that might be useful for future researchers.

NAGPRA has contributed to osteology in that the analyses produced as a result of cultural affiliation studies are more comprehensive and consistent than ever before, because osteologists might never get the opportunity to restudy the material. Thirdly, the cultural affiliation requirements of NAGPRA might require further research than has been done in the past. Thus, rather than decreasing the amount of osteological study, the law might actually serve to increase it.

And, while there is a general tendency for American Indians to be wary of individuals who work with skeletal remains, there are some Native Americans who are themselves involved with skeletons for specific reasons. Dorothy Lippert, a Choctaw archaeologist who works at the Repatriation Office of the Smithsonian Institution's National Museum of Natural History, has participated in human skeletal analysis. Her reasons for studying American Indian skeletons are different from those of most other biological anthropologists or osteologists. It is her opinion that she is able to provide breath to the dead, so that she can help them tell their stories to the living. She states: "For many of our ancestors, skeletal analysis is one of the only ways that they are able to tell us their stories. The forthcoming information may not be as clear as it is from other sources; it seems that it is difficult to speak with a voice made of bone."[8]

On the other hand, Jack Trope, the director of the American Association for Indian Affairs, and Walter Echo-Hawk, a senior staff attorney with NARF, recognize that repatriation "is a part of a larger historical tragedy: the failure of the United States Government, and other institutions, to understand and respect the spiritual and cultural beliefs and practices of Native people. Governmental policies that threaten Native American religions are not merely historical anachronisms but continue to have a devastating impact on contemporary Native Americans."[9]

Ultimately, it is expected that the biological-anthropological enterprise will become more ethical and fair to the dead, although there is a likelihood of a continued or increased use of the dead for political purposes, such as custody and reburial of skeletons and control over the data and interpretations based on skeletal remains. It is only when equal treatment has occurred that American Indians will feel they have protected their ancestors.

5

Repatriation and Museums

The Colville Tribe is not against science.
We are against the use of science to discriminate
and disenfranchise Native American tribes.[10]
—Marla Big Boy, Colville tribe attorney

WHAT ARE MUSEUMS?

Museums are places where special collections are held for the benefit of all people. Some museums maintain collections of fossils, rocks, minerals, and other objects related to the natural world. Other museums hold collections of everyday items made by cultures around the globe. Still other museums house collections of art created by some of the greatest artists of all time. Regardless of the subjects, museums exist as educational institutions whose primary purpose is the collection, protection, and educational use of specific types of objects.

Museums have had a special history of growth, tied in many ways to the cultures of which they are a part, as well as the society within which they flourish. In Europe, for example, the Age of Exploration brought with it a growing number of encounters between Europeans and other cultures. People returning from trips to the so-called "New World" often brought back with them tales of cultures so different from their own that they were obliged to provide evidence of those civilizations in the form of souvenirs, drawings, and, occasionally, even representatives of the people themselves. Generally, these souvenirs were kept within the walls of palaces and sometimes monasteries, but as society grew more open and democratic during the Industrial Revolution of the nineteenth century, these objects and the information about them became more accessible to the general population. Private collections—"cabinets of curiosities"—shifted from private to public or government ownership, and museums opened to the common people.

Some of these royal collections were old, made up of items of tribute given to kings, exotic items collected from foreign expeditions, and other goods seized as a royal right. When museums took on these royal collections, they also took on the responsibilities of maintaining them, providing education about them, protecting them, and classifying them into some sort of order for ease of exhibition. As the number of specimens grew, and scientific interest in them grew, so, too, did the public interest in them. More and more museums became public institutions over time, and, as such, they were expected to take part in the development of public education. This required museums to do more than fulfill their traditional role of providing learning or research opportunities. Museums also entered the realm of imparting an understanding of what was "normal" and what was not.

Museums gradually shifted the focus of their purpose away from the scientific public who relied on museum collections for research and more toward entertaining the general public

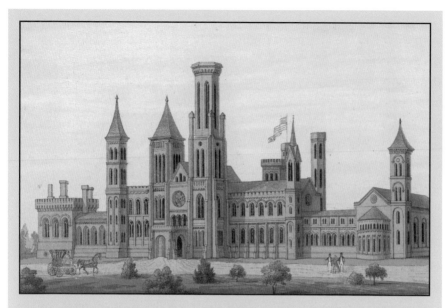

The Smithsonian Institution, located in Washington, D.C., was founded in 1846 and is today the largest museum in the world. The museum focuses on scholarship, housing a large collection of art and cultural objects, as well as natural science objects.

with exotic items from other cultures often perceived as "otherworldly." Michael Ames, in a book that looks at the history and changing roles of museums, offers a comparison of two separate facilities—the Smithsonian Institution of Washington, D.C., and the American Museum in New York City—and the contributions each made in the evolution of the modern museum. Both of these institutions were important in the mid-nineteenth century, yet only the Smithsonian still exists today.

The Smithsonian Museum of Natural History came into being in 1846 as the result of a bequest from an Englishman named James Smithson. It was established to increase knowledge among people. The American Museum in New York City, on the other hand, was bought and maintained by P.T. Barnum, a famous American entrepreneur and showman. To Barnum, the museum was solely a business venture.

The Smithsonian Institution maintains collections of rocks, insects, dead animals, plants, and fossils, as well as pieces of art and artifacts created by both modern cultures and long-dead ones. The museum has continued to maintain an active program of research, public education, collection, and scientific publication.

By contrast, the American Museum of New York City (which was destroyed by a fire in 1865) held a collection of curiosities, serpents, whales, elephants, hippos, wolves, buffalo, as well as circus performers, such as midgets, bearded ladies, tattooed men, jugglers, and other "attractions." Where the Smithsonian concerned itself with scholarship, Barnum's American Museum chose razzle-dazzle; where the Smithsonian was conservative, the American Museum was flamboyant; where the Smithsonian operated quietly with grants of public funds, the American Museum was run on a profit gained from admission fees.

In contrasting the two institutions, Ames brings up the dilemma that confronts museums today—should a museum be a place of scientific research or a wildly popular public attraction? Is it possible for a museum to be both at the same time, or must the museum focus on attracting visitors (as Barnum did), to the detriment of the serious researcher?

Although the primary function of museums is to exhibit their specimens, they also serve to display (and influence) the public image of the community within which they are located. A museum can express the image of the community either directly (by promoting and affirming the dominant values of the community) or indirectly (by subordinating or rejecting alternative views). It is this role as a producer of public image that causes American Indians' discontent with museums today.

To some people, museums are nothing more than storage facilities that hold glass cases built to house artifacts from cultures long thought to be dead or dying. In the 1880s, museums generally displayed items from "primitive" cultures (including

American Indians, Pacific Islanders, and South American tribes) within a natural history context, as if the cultures were so much a part of nature that they might be considered specimens alongside animals—curiosities on a par with African elephants or Tasmanian devils. Also, as researchers returned from their fieldwork with more and more examples of objects made by these exotic cultures, more exhibits were needed to show off the cultures, the materials, and the research of the scientists.

Preparing exhibits requires scientific research as well as an artistic touch, and the museum professionals who develop exhibits are well trained in the work they do. However, as the exhibits take on a life of their own, the museum (and the museum professional) eventually becomes the self-appointed keeper of another's material and the self-appointed interpreter of another's history. It is the exhibit that shapes the public's perception about an object and the culture that produced that object. In truth, as strange as it may seem, the person who writes the text for the exhibit has the capacity to influence more people than the cultural group that the display is about. In this manner, the museum becomes the "expert" and the cultural group becomes almost unnecessary.

It was mentioned earlier how the museum can influence the public image of the community in which it is located, but a museum can just as easily influence the public's image of a particular cultural group. This can be done directly (through a representation of the group as "primitive," "savage," or "warlike"), or indirectly (by refusing to portray a certain culture in a modern setting). This representation of cultures, in conjunction with the interpretation of the material within a museum's collection, can contribute to the public's perception of cultures in a negative manner.

An additional responsibility of museums, in conjunction with their role as educational facilities, is to maintain and protect the objects within their collections for future visitors and researchers alike. Since the collections are the heart and soul of

In addition to serving to educate the public, museums are also responsible for maintaining and protecting the objects in their collections. Shown here is a kachina doll display at the Southwest Museum of the American Indian in Los Angeles, which has one of the nation's largest collections of American Indian cultural objects. Many of these objects are sacred to American Indians and they believe that museums should return them.

museums, it is necessary that they be protected, preserved, or conserved. Specially trained museum professionals are responsible for ensuring that the items in the collection are free from pests or other things that could be detrimental to the artifact, as well as finding ways of preventing certain classes of artifacts from being harmed by storage, handling, or other practices.

Different types of artifacts or other items in a museum collection require different methods of treatment. Some artifacts made of animal skins (or even stuffed animals themselves) require treatment with pesticides to keep insects from destroying them, as do materials like feathers, woolen weavings, and even wooden items. Other types of artifacts (such as stone items, minerals, and so forth) are more durable and require only that they be protected from being dropped or smashed. Each item within a collection requires a particular method of protection, and museums are expected to keep them in relatively good condition for the future.

American Indians' Relationships with Museums

In general, indigenous populations throughout the world have not been represented very well by museums. In the United States, for example, museums such as the Smithsonian Institution, the Chicago Field Museum, and the Southwest Museum in Los Angeles have not represented the cultures of the American Indian tribes in the same manner that they have represented non-Indian cultures from the same periods of history. Why is this?

In the 1880s and 1890s, anthropologists and historians thought that American Indians were destined to disappear, to become more like Anglo-Americans. These professionals thought it was their duty not only to preserve the traditional culture before it died (conducting field research to record information on the tribal groups) but also to preserve the material culture that made up the everyday objects that Indians used. Some of the materials were collected in improper ways (such as the removal from Indian graves of human skeletal remains and associated items buried with the bodies) and others were purchased from unscrupulous people who might have stolen them. A few artifacts were collected directly from Indians who were coerced into giving up the items by anthropologists who thought it was more important to have the object than to worry about the methods of getting it. One individual, Frank Cushing, while on a collecting expedition to the pueblo of Zuñi, would force his way into secret ceremonies, threaten to harm those who would not let him in, and then try to participate as if he had been invited. He bought numerous artifacts from anyone who would sell them to him, and the items were then shipped back to the American Museum of Natural History in New York City, where they reside today.

The general impression that American Indians get from the way they are represented in museums is that of static, dead cultures that ceased to exist in the late 1800s and can now only be found in the minds of anthropologists or in museum collections. Is it any wonder that American Indians often see museums as a sort of mausoleum—a place where the dead are taken to be prodded, measured, displayed, labeled, and finally put away into storage? These dead may be humans (human skeletal remains, bits and pieces of humans such as scalps) or objects made dead by their removal from the culture that gave them life.

A second concern American Indians have regarding museums is the public image that museum exhibits have helped form. As mentioned, museum exhibits contribute to the public's perception of tribal groups, and many exhibits focus on particular aspects of tribal culture. The focus—either in the past or in the present—can depend upon the research orientation of the person who plans the exhibit, the materials within the collection, or perhaps a historical event or personage. More commonly, American Indians are presented in the past, as a part of a local or regional "history." This has two adverse effects: It continues to give the impression that Indians exist only in the past, and it allows the museum to control the history of the tribal culture rather than allowing the tribe to control its own history.

Finally, many American Indian groups also feel uncomfortable being the source or subject of other people's education. As noted before, one of the primary roles of museums is to educate the public. Museums whose specialty is American Indian materials, by the very nature of their collections, are educating people about what it means (or meant) to be "Indian." This sets the museum up as the expert and relegates living Native people to a secondary role in teaching about their own culture.

Museums, Repatriation, and Human Remains

In chapter 4, some of the reasons that anthropologists wish to store human remains (not just American Indian human remains) in museum collections were addressed. The biological anthropologists Landau and Steele made some good arguments about the utility of human remains for study. However, American Indians have long held beliefs that humans should not be disturbed from their places of interment and that, if they must be disturbed, they should be returned to their original burial place (or as near it as possible) as soon as the research is completed.

During the 1970s, various federal agencies had "in-house" policies that dealt with human remains. As mentioned in chapter 3, the Department of the Interior maintained a "Policy for the Disposition of Human Remains" that served as a model for most other federal agencies involved with archaeological research. The policy called for the reburial of materials (after study) only when direct kinship or ethnic affinity to an individual could be demonstrated.

However, not all human remains of American Indian ancestry were removed to museums and storage areas. An archaeologist and a physical anthropologist working in Idaho analyzed and then reburied skeletal remains found during construction of a water and sewage line and during a cemetery relocation project. Both projects involved the Nez Perce tribe. In the cemetery relocation project, the graves were located and excavated by teams of university archaeologists and tribal members working together, and the skeletal remains were analyzed by physical anthropologists and then reburied on tribal land. Needless to say, however, this incident of reburial of

American Indian human remains was the exception rather than the rule.

Eventually, however, after twenty years of debate, the passage of NAGPRA and the NMAIA repatriation legislation increased the likelihood that human remains would be repatriated to American Indian tribes, despite continued opposition by some anthropologists because of their desire for unfettered scientific inquiry. Some tribes have been able to get sets of human remains back from museums, among them the Cheyenne tribe of Oklahoma and the Larsen Bay community of Kodiak Island in the Gulf of Alaska.

The Cheyenne Request

On April 25, 1993, Cheyenne chiefs and societies met to sign a formal document addressed to the Smithsonian Institution requesting the skeletal remains of any Cheyenne individuals within the museum's collections. Three weeks later, the director of the Repatriation Office of the Smithsonian met with the chiefs in Oklahoma to initiate the formal repatriation process for eighteen sets of human remains that were then part of the museum's holdings.

Since the museum policy of maintaining collections in accordance with preservation standards would have required that the human remains be packed in bubble wrap and Styrofoam© pellets for shipment to the tribe, the Cheyenne chiefs selected a number of individuals to travel to Washington, D.C., to prepare the remains for reburial.

The remains belonged to victims of the Sand Creek Massacre of November 29, 1864, an incident in which soldiers of the Third Colorado Volunteers, under the command of Colonel John M. Chivington, attacked a peaceful band of Cheyennes and Arapahos who were camped along Big Sandy Creek in southeastern Colorado. Accounts of the massacre told of how the soldiers fired on unarmed men, women, and children who had been promised peace and protection. Further

This plaque, near the state capitol in Denver, Colorado, commemorates the Sand Creek Massacre, which was a brutal attack by the Third Colorado Volunteers on a camp of defenseless Arapahos and Cheyennes in November 1864. Several Cheyenne victims of the massacre were taken to the Smithsonian Institution, where they were studied by scientists. In 1993, the remains of these victims were repatriated to the Cheyenne people of Oklahoma, who buried them in Concho Cemetery, Oklahoma.

accounts tell of the mutilations that were performed on the Indian dead and dying. In all, more than one hundred Indian women and children were killed, along with twenty-eight Indian men.

The Cheyenne men and women who went to the Smithsonian to prepare the bodies for transportation back to Oklahoma wrapped the human remains in buckskin and Pendleton blankets and then placed them in specially made cedar boxes with cedar shavings for packing and protection. The human remains were then sent to the Oklahoma Historical

Society in Oklahoma City before being reburied in Concho Cemetery, Oklahoma.

The repatriation, according to Connie Hart Yellowman, one of the participants, provided tribal members with a visible, positive example of how a group of people can work together to reach a common goal. It also allowed members of the younger generation to witness certain rarely performed ceremonies conducted by elders. When the last set of human remains had been placed in the specially prepared graves, and when the last Cheyenne tribal member had placed a handful of dirt over the boxes, the eighteen victims of the Sand Creek Massacre had been brought home and laid to rest.

The Larsen Bay Request

In 1987, the residents of Larsen Bay, on Kodiak Island in the Gulf of Alaska, submitted a formal request to the Smithsonian Institution for the return of human burial remains removed from the Uyak site by Aleš Hrdlička (a physical anthropologist who lived from 1869 to 1943) in the 1930s. The Larsen Bay request involved the return of more than 750 sets of human remains, representing approximately 1,000 individuals and 95 lots of associated funerary objects.

The repatriation process began with the Larsen Bay community's request for the return of the material. Since the request was made before the passage of the National Museum of the American Indian Act, the Smithsonian was reluctant to repatriate the remains to individuals who were not lineal descendants of the humans represented by the human skeletal remains. The Smithsonian later suggested that it would repatriate the remains of all historic graves to the community, but the community pressed for the return of all skeletal material that had been excavated from the site. The scientists argued that the residents of the Larsen Bay community might be related to the historic materials but were not likely descendants of the ancient remains. The representatives of the community argued that all individuals from

Kodiak Island should be considered their ancestors and relatives, and they wished to reclaim all material from Kodiak Island that was part of the Smithsonian's collections.

At first, the center of the conflict revolved around the so-called "cultural affiliation" of the human remains, and whether the Larsen Bay community had the right to request repatriation. Both the Larsen Bay community and the Smithsonian hired outside experts to examine the relationships between the contemporary community and the archaeological remains, but both sets of experts came up with different answers. Ultimately, however, the secretary of the Smithsonian Institution agreed to repatriate the remains to the Larsen Bay community. The Smithsonian Institution transferred the remains to Kodiak Island in early September 1991, and, on October 5, 1991, they were reburied near the site from which they had been dug up.

The Larsen Bay case is significant to the different groups involved in the repatriation but for different reasons and on different levels. To scientists, the repatriation is important because it represents the return of items that might not be "culturally affiliated" with the contemporary group of Alaskans. To the residents of the Larsen Bay community, it is significant because it allowed them to lay to rest the people they considered their ancestors. To members of the larger legal community, it sets a legal precedence because it shows that tribal groups have been granted legal rights to human remains once thought to be the property of museums and other facilities.

It is necessary to note at this point that not all American Indian groups wish to obtain the skeletal material now held in museums and other collections. The Zuñi Tribal Council issued a resolution in 1989 that asked museums and other institutions to care for and curate any Zuñi ancestral human remains that they might have in their possession. In the tribal view, the human remains have been desecrated by their removal, and there are no adequate measures to reverse or mitigate that desecration.

Museums, Repatriation, and Cultural Artifacts

In 1970, the Onondaga tribe began trying to regain wampum belts held within a museum in New York State. The tribe's attempt to get back these sensitive cultural items met with widespread comment, not only in local and national newspapers, such as the *Watertown* (NY) *Daily Times* and *Akwesasne Notes* (a national American Indian newspaper), but also in scholarly journals, such as the American Anthropological Association's newsletter.

Of course, anthropologists were on both sides of the issue. Some came out in support of the return of the cultural artifacts to the tribes, while others spoke out against such a return. The Onondagas were eventually able to retrieve their sacred wampum belts when the New York State Assembly voted in favor of their return, but only after the tribe constructed a special museum for the belts' protection and curation. The battle over the control of the artifacts was more than just an attempt to regain a single set of artifacts—it caused many museum professionals and archaeologists to reexamine the relationship between museums and the people whose cultural artifacts the museums exhibit. American Indians, it seemed, were no longer content to allow museums to continue to determine what was to be displayed, how the material was to be interpreted, and the limits of Indian involvement in the entire preservation process.

Some museum professionals reacted to the repatriation of the material with shock, but others were more in touch with the problems inherent in museums. In 1971, Dr. James D. Nason, then curator of ethnology at the Thomas Burke Memorial Washington State Museum at the University of Washington, outlined three basic criticisms that he had heard American Indian groups make against museums: that some or all of the materials within museums had been collected in the past by either immoral or illicit means; that collections were developed to satisfy materialistic greed or cultural imperialism; and that museums seek to maintain collections in such a way that Indians are excluded from any contact with or relationship with their material heritage.

Nason went on to outline certain conditions that he felt should be met before any cultural material was returned to indigenous peoples. Among these was that the items be culturally significant, that an adequate facility be available for their storage and protection, that trained personnel and stabilized funding be available, and that the materials revert to museum stewardship should any of the other conditions not be met.

Despite changes in the attitudes of museum personnel, not all American Indians were content to wait quietly for museums to return items of importance to them or to change patterns of exhibiting Indian culture. In 1971, members of various American Indian tribes protested at the Southwest Museum in Los Angeles over the display of American Indian human skeletal remains and the exhibit of what tribal members considered sacred items. Many of the Indian protesters were arrested, but their demonstration proved a point. Eventually, the American Association of Museums, the national organization for museums, made it a policy that no human remains should be exhibited within any of its member museums.

Other museum professionals who were interested in the relationships between American Indian groups and the "business" of museums provided discussions about dealing with the desires of Native groups for the return of materials in museum collections and trying to find positive ways in which museums could become involved with living Indians, rather than confining their efforts to retrieving cultural items from the nineteenth century.

While museum professionals were writing about the relationships between Indian groups and museums, Indian tribes also began to provide their perspectives on those relationships. The Zuñis made it known that their involvement with the management of sacred cultural resources was making sure that the people responsible for the religious artifacts participate in the decisions made about them, and that when a conflict exists between the religious use of an artifact and its scientific or artistic use, the religious value supersedes all others.

In the 1980s, the Zuñi tribe was notified that one of its *Ahayu:da* was being offered for sale in a public auction. The *Ahayu:da* are twin deities of great power, associated with prowess and physical skill. They are viewed as protectors of the Zuñi people. Their images are represented by cylindrical wood sculptures and are used at certain ceremonies and at particular times of the year. The "new" *Ahayu:da* are placed at two of a series of shrines surrounding Zuñi Pueblo and the old ones placed on a pile of "retired" ones to naturally disintegrate and return to the earth.

The Zuñis claimed that *Ahayu:da* are community owned, and no one has the right to move them from their shrines. In addition, since no one has the right to sell them to another individual, all *Ahayu:da* in private or museum collections must have been stolen. The Zuñis, therefore, requested that any *Ahayu:da* found in museums or private collections be given back to them so that they could be returned to the shrines.

The success of the Zuñi tribe in getting back the *Ahayu:da* is, in large part, based on its approach, which stressed gentle persuasion rather than confrontation. Since the beginning of the Zuñis' repatriation efforts, more than eighty *Ahayu:da* have been returned to Zuñi, and the tribe expects its efforts to continue to meet with success as more *Ahayu:da* are discovered in private or museum collections.

Repatriation and the Future of Museums

In addition to the conflict over the return of certain classes of artifacts to tribal groups, there is also a clash over how artifacts should be valued. In general, there is often disagreement between the museum perspective, which values the artifact for its ability to provide information about the past or about people of the past, and the American Indian perspective, which assigns value to the artifact's ability to help a culture preserve its traditions or heritage. Museums often define "heritage" based on the products of a culture (the material objects), while American Indians often define heritage as the culture itself, the processes rather than the products.

Additionally, some Indians view museums as places where items are held captive. These items might have been taken from the tribe in various ways, but are important as much for the traditions associated with the objects as the physical object itself. The value of the objects lies not in their artistic or technological value, but with their meaning for the tribal group. To the tribe, it is more important that certain objects be used rather than that they be preserved in the museum conservator's way.

In addition, there is often conflict between a conservator's ethic of preserving cultural items and tribal perspectives that cultural items should be allowed to naturally disintegrate. As the Zuñi example concerning the *Ahayu:da* mentioned, some types of cultural items were originally meant to be allowed to decompose so that they would return to the earth. Some cultural groups also believe that particular cultural items are alive and should be fed, given access to fresh air, and be renewed at certain times. These ideas conflict with the museum's requirements for protection of the cultural items from contamination and fluctuations in heat, humidity, and light as a means of prolonging the "life" of the items.

In Australia, some museum personnel have noted that the request for repatriation of cultural items by local indigenous populations did not always result in the wholesale decimation of collections, as feared by museum professionals. Christopher Anderson, in dealing with the Aborigines of southern Australia, found that, following the development of social networks between the Aborigines and museum professionals, Aboriginal people actually loaned more objects to the South Australian Museum in Adelaide for protection, storage, and/or safekeeping. Additionally, they sometimes were able to provide more information about other cultural items.

Do museums have a future? Repatriation of human remains and special classes of cultural items will not lead to the depletion of museum collections and force museums to close their doors, but museums will need to change their function in order to continue operating in the future. Museums will need to follow aspects of the P.T. Barnum school of entertainment, as well as the Smithsonian school of education. In addition, museums will need to understand that there is conflict between the Western concept of museums as protectors of cultural items of the past and the American Indian notion that the people are the protectors of their own culture.

6

Summary of Repatriation Issues

. . . (traditional cultural properties') significance cannot be determined solely by historians, ethnographers, ethnohistorians, ethnobotanists, and other professionals. The significance of traditional cultural properties must be determined by the community that values them.[11]
—Patricia Parker

So far, we have discussed the reasons for repatriation and the legal history and guidelines of the two major repatriation laws. We've looked at the way that the repatriation acts impact various aspects of anthropology, as well as the way that the repatriation movement affects museums. We have also indirectly discussed how repatriation impacts American Indians as we have looked at American Indian claims for repatriation, American Indian relationships with museums, and American Indian attitudes toward the objects within museum collections themselves.

Though biological anthropologists believe that keeping skeletal material in museums is important in studying the origins and makeup of Native people, American Indians have successfully won the right to return their ancestors to their homeland. Shown here is a group of Haidas dancing at the Field Museum in Chicago after the museum returned 150 of the tribe's ancestors to their care.

In this chapter, some of the concerns that American Indian tribes have in regard to the laws that are supposed to return special items to them will be discussed. Among these issues are the continued scientific study of human remains; the application of repatriation statutes to extremely old material (for example, Kennewick); the problems presented by culturally unidentifiable human remains; the remains of nonfederally recognized tribes; materials found on private land; and the return of materials that are important to particular members within a tribe but are not classified as "tribal sacred items" or "items of cultural patrimony."

PERCEIVED INADEQUACIES OF REPATRIATION LAWS

The Continued Study of Human Remains

NAGPRA does not authorize the initiation of new scientific studies, but it does not preclude such research when a museum deems it necessary for determining the cultural affiliation of a set of human remains. Additionally, the law allows for the continuation of studies when the human remains under examination are indispensable for the completion of a specific scientific study, the outcome of which would be of major benefit to the United States. The key word in this statement is *completion*. Technically this wording would suggest that in order for the study to continue, it must already be under way prior to the time that the final identification of the tribe to which the materials were to be repatriated is identified.

Many tribes are concerned about this, believing the law provides an apparent authorization for study prior to repatriation. Scientists and museums argue that it is often necessary for human remains to be studied so that cultural affiliation may be determined or so that repatriation to the most appropriate descendants or tribe can be carried out. Tribes require that the role of scientific study in this determination be clarified, asking that NAGPRA be amended to provide more restrictive guidelines on this issue. They want the law to state explicitly that where existing documentation establishes geographic location and cultural affiliation by clear, reasonable belief, or by a preponderance of evidence, no scientific studies of any kind will be allowed on ancestral skeletal remains.

The Application of Repatriation Statutes to Extremely Old Material

The court case over the Kennewick Man illustrates one of the problems that came about after repatriation legislation was passed. In a case like Kennewick, where a set of human remains is so old that no one tribe can demonstrate a clear cultural affiliation to it, should scientists be permitted to study the material, especially if the remains would be essential for a continuing study, the outcome of which would be beneficial to the United States? Would the study of the first inhabitants of North and South America be considered "beneficial" to the United States?

Representatives of the scientists suing for the right to conduct scientific research on Kennewick Man argue that the repatriation laws (NAGPRA specifically, in the case of Kennewick Man) were not meant to apply to remains as old as those of Kennewick. They argue that such remains, by the very nature of their age, cannot be assigned to any one tribe, or, more specifically, that no single tribe can demonstrate cultural affiliation with a set of human remains so old.

Should "Pan-Indianism," the belief that all American Indians are culturally interrelated at some point and that the problems of any American Indian group is a matter of concern for all living American Indian groups, play any role in this debate? Should any Indian tribe be able to claim and rebury human remains if no other tribe wishes to do so? Should the scientific perspective be given equal consideration with American Indian religious perspectives?

The Problems with "Culturally Unidentifiable Human Remains"

Another inadequacy identified in the law is NAGPRA's failure to protect "culturally unidentifiable human remains," something the NAGPRA Review Committee has tried to remedy through recommendations that have yet to be codified. Section 7 of NAGPRA concerns Native American human remains and funerary objects whose cultural affiliation has not been established through inventories or summaries prepared by museums. Tribal groups, among them the Gila River Indian Community at Sacaton, Arizona, and the Standing Rock Sioux Tribe of Fort Yates, North Dakota, have repatriated human remains that could not specifically be identified as belonging to their tribe, because they felt a tie to the remains as American

Indians. Even the NAGPRA Review Committee saw this issue as a point of frustration.

In 1997, Washington State representative to Congress Richard "Doc" Hastings introduced a bill that would have amended NAGPRA to require certain levels of study prior to repatriating "culturally unidentifiable human remains." The law would have made it much easier for scientists to gain study access to any unaffiliated material and also required that cultural affiliation be documented to a much greater extent. The National Congress of American Indians opposed the proposed changes.

In 1998, the NAGPRA Review Committee issued a set of Draft Principles of Agreement Regarding the Disposition of Culturally Unidentifiable Human Remains, but the principles only presented guidelines for the ultimate disposition of these types of remains. Nothing has been codified in the regulations that are used to implement the law, and scientists and American Indian perspectives on the issue continue to be almost diametrically opposed.

Repatriation of the Remains of Nonfederally Recognized Tribes

American Indian views on this issue are divided but for differing reasons. Many Indians feel that nonfederally recognized tribes are no less Indian than their federally recognized counterparts. Others are afraid that to allow unrecognized tribes equal standing under NAGPRA would allow such groups to bypass the normally tedious process of federal recognition.

The difference between a federally recognized Indian tribe and a nonfederally recognized Indian tribe is one of political relationship with the federal government. In the past, the federal government tried to "terminate" Indian tribes. Some tribes voted to terminate under the U.S. government's proposals and were essentially disbanded. Other tribes chose to reorganize into different political structures that blended some of their traditional forms of government with more American

Many Native groups, including those who live in Alaska, have been denied sovereignty by the U.S. government and thus have not been extended repatriation rights under NAGPRA. Shown here is a group of Alaska Natives during the fifth-annual "We the People" march through downtown Anchorage in August 2002. The rally is held in support of obtaining sovereignty from the U.S. government.

governmental systems. Those tribes that chose to terminate lost their recognition as domestic, dependent nations by the U.S. government.

Today, the tribes that maintained their own traditional government are considered "federally recognized" and are entitled to receive benefits from the U.S. government based on this distinction. Tribal groups that either lost their recognition or have not been able to prove to the Bureau of Indian Affairs (BIA) that they are, indeed, separate and distinct nations or communities, are considered nonfederally recognized tribal groups. Some states, such as Alabama and Oklahoma, recognize tribal groups within state boundaries and maintain special relationships with them, but state recognition does not confer the same benefits as federal recognition. The NAGPRA Review Committee noted a need to find a way to permit Native American groups that are not presently recognized by the BIA to repatriate their human remains, funerary objects, sacred items, or objects of cultural patrimony.

While all tribes agree that human remains of unrecognized American Indian groups are, have been, and always will be American Indian, many are concerned about extending rights to all Native groups under NAGPRA. In a statement prepared for the March 1997 Review Committee meeting in Oklahoma, seven tribes from southwestern Oklahoma—the Apache tribe of Oklahoma, the Caddo tribe, the Comanche tribe, the Delaware tribe of western Oklahoma, the Fort Sill Apache, the Kiowa, and the Wichita and Affiliated tribes—felt that repatriation should apply only to federally recognized groups. Though they believed that human remains, regardless of affiliation, should not be left in museums, they expressed a concern that to repatriate human remains to nonfederally recognized tribes could potentially assign rights and authority to groups that have come into existence without a legitimate claim of historical continuity. The working group felt that culturally unidentifiable human remains should be repatriated to the federally recognized tribes on whose aboriginal lands the remains were found, with the review committee making decisions in cases where multiple tribes claimed the same ancestral lands.

While no specific remedies are defined for every case, they do offer suggestions for disposition in cases where the human remains are associated with a nonfederally recognized tribe. They suggest regional consultations that might prove beneficial in situations where the human remains represent a population for which there are no present-day cultural survivors or where the present-day cultural survivors are members of nonfederally recognized Indian tribes.

The Concern with Materials on Private Land

Another shortcoming of NAGPRA is its ability to protect human remains on private land. Many American Indian groups question why the graves protection portion of NAGPRA was not applied to all lands within the United States rather than just to federal or tribal lands. At least thirty-four states have burial protection laws, both relatively recent as well as historic or older, and these laws typically prohibit the intentional disturbance of unmarked graves. Many of the laws also provide guidelines to protect the graves and mandate disposition of human remains from the graves in a way that guarantees reburial after a period of study.

If such state laws designed to protect human remains have been upheld as constitutionally valid, it raises a question as to why NAGPRA was not applied to all lands. The National Congress of American Indians has called for changes in NAGPRA to extend protection of funerary remains and objects on all lands, wherever they might be located, within the exterior boundaries of the United States.

Why is extension of NAGPRA important? According to a study of American archaeologists, approximately 49 percent of archaeologists work either within the U.S. government, the private sector, or in a museum setting. If one assumes that private sector and museum archaeologists are as closely tied to federal regulations as their government counterparts, then NAGPRA or the NMAIA affects the research of only about half of all American archaeologists. Academic archaeologists, those more often participating in "pure research," are less confined by federal regulations, and they make up 35 percent of the survey population. When these archaeologists conduct research on federal or tribal lands, their research is covered under NAGPRA, as are the artifacts that they might collect. However, if their research is conducted on private land, they are less constrained. Although the artifacts they collect might eventually come under control of NAGPRA (if the museums that curate the artifacts receive federal funds), their initial excavations may not be as stringently controlled.

The ascription of property rights to archaeological resources is, as archaeologist Ruthann Knudson notes, "a complicated legal, as well as social, issue."[12] While human remains may be protected under various state laws, federal intervention on private land can sometimes be perceived as a violation of the "takings clause" of the Fifth Amendment to the Constitution if the landowner is in any way denied access or free use of his property without adequate compensation.

Under NAGPRA, the excavation of Native American human remains and objects must follow the Archaeological Resources Protection Act of 1979 (ARPA), but tribal authority under this law is limited. If the tribe has the power to issue antiquities permits for the land where the remains are located, it may refuse to grant a permit and thereby prevent excavation. But if the tribe has no such authority, its options are limited. ARPA requires only that consultation with the tribe occur, not that the tribe actually has to grant permission for the excavations to be carried out. Additionally, if the tribes are to have the right of ownership and control as called for under NAGPRA, the artifacts become tribal property only *after* the scientist is finished removing and/or studying them—not before.

Tribes have even less authority in the case of an inadvertent discovery of human remains on federal land if there are no known or easily discovered lineal descendants. If the material cannot be reasonably identified with a particular tribe, then the material becomes the "property" of the tribe that has the closest cultural affiliation with the material and makes a claim for it. Of course, scientific study of the material might be needed to determine which group has the "closest" affiliation, something the tribes may not want, but something to which the tribes may be forced to agree in order to regain the human remains for reburial.

Ultimately, it can happen that no tribe may be judged to be

an aboriginal occupant of the land as defined through a final judgment of the Indian Claims Commission or the U.S. Court of Claims. It might also happen that no tribe will be viewed as being culturally affiliated with the materials as defined under NAGPRA. Both of these conditions occurred in the case of Kennewick Man.

Satanta's Shield

There are certain objects within museum collections that were once the property of particular Indian individuals but do not easily fall within the definition of "sacred" items or "objects of cultural patrimony." A quick example might make this easier to understand.

A Kiowa war chief named Satanta had a war shield that was given to him for his protection in battle (it protected him in more than one hundred battles). The shield hung in the Kiowa medicine lodge, and Satanta proudly displayed it after every battle for the Kiowa people to see. Even though the shield did not have a specific role in the practice of the Kiowa Sun Dance, the last Sun Dance of the Kiowa was delayed until the shield could be brought from its home to its place of honor.

Before Satanta was taken to Texas for imprisonment, he gave the shield to his son, Gray Goose, who kept it until he died. Supposedly, under the terms of Gray Goose's will, the shield was given to the superintendent of the Anadarko Agency of the Bureau of Indian Affairs. After a while, the shield made its way to a prominent museum in northern California, where the family eventually located it. The museum had a valid right to ownership, as indicated by the original accessions records.

The shield is not sacred under the definition of NAGPRA, because it never had a formal role within the tribe's traditional religion, except within the practice of religion by an individual tribal member (Satanta). Neither is the shield an object of cultural patrimony under the definition of NAGPRA, because it was individually owned property that could be legally disposed of (sold or given away) by the owner. However, the shield is both sacred and an object of cultural patrimony to the Kiowa tribe and the family. It is believed to possess powers that were given it by its maker, and it was a part of the tribal cultural inventory relating to the Indian Wars of the 1860s and 1870s, as well as an important object related to one of the last war chiefs of the Kiowas.

There are additional problems. The descendants of Satanta were reluctant to request the return of the shield under NAG-PRA because they did not want the shield to go to the Kiowa tribe for fear of its theft. Additionally, the family recognized that the museum had a legal claim to ownership of the shield based on the donation documents, but they questioned whether the museum's ownership was "moral."

Eventually, a compromise was worked out. The museum sent the shield on permanent loan to the Fort Sill Museum in Fort Sill, Oklahoma, where family members can more easily visit it. The original museum still technically maintains ownership of the shield, but the family does not have to fly to California to see it. The shield can still play an important role in the Kiowa family's history, even if it does not reside within their home.

Repatriation, American Indians, Et Al

Has repatriation led to the destruction of museums or the end of anthropology? Has repatriation given the tribes back all of their special items? Has everyone been happy with the progress that has been made since the passage of the two repatriation laws in 1989 and 1990? A resounding *no* is the answer to all these questions.

Contrary to the fears of members of the scientific and museum communities, repatriation has not led to the destruction of anthropology or the wholesale gutting of museums. It has perhaps led to a series of inconveniences between the disciplines and American Indians, but it has also led to the formation of some strong partnerships that have proven beneficial to all.

Museums have been placed in a situation where financial concerns have risen by virtue of the need to inventory all of their collections to determine whether they possessed items that were covered under NAGPRA. At the same time, these inventories have also proven to be a blessing in that they have forced museums to identify any deficiencies in their records or any gaps in their collections.

American Indians have benefited from the repatriation laws in various ways. Some tribes have been able to regain the remains of their ancestors for reburial (or, in some instances, initial burial). This has lessened the social hardships experienced by some tribes. Other tribes, such as the Zuñi and the Onondaga, have been able to regain ownership and control over items of cultural importance to their people. Additionally, museums and American Indians have developed a sort of uneasy truce concerning collections and ethnographic information provided in museum displays.

What remains to be done in the quest for repatriation? There are some areas in which American Indians feel NAGPRA and NMAIA are deficient. Many of those issues have already been discussed, but other issues will likely arise in the future. Those involved hope that, through careful consideration of the history of repatriation and the ongoing struggle to find a middle ground where all interested parties can meet, repatriation will prove to be of some benefit to everyone it affects.

7

Reclaiming Physical Heritage: Sacred Sites

. . . the centre of the Native American religious system is the affirmation that spiritual power is infused throughout the environment in general, as well as at interconnected special places, and that knowledgeable people are participants in that power.[13]
—Dorothy Theodoratus and Frank LaPena

Most people and their families have places that have special meaning to them—places where their parents were born, or places where their grandparents lived. For many Americans, those special places might be somewhere else. People whose ancestors migrated to the United States might have been told about "the old country," or maybe you've heard stories about where your great-grandparents lived. All of us have what is called "attachment to place." This means that geography has an impact on us personally. Many people may feel this kind of an attachment to their hometown.

The U.S. government has historically had a government-to-government relationship with Indian tribes, which was established through the signing of treaties. Shown here is a typical nineteenth-century depiction of the first treaty between the Delawares and William Penn in 1682.

For American Indians, there is also an attachment to place, one that has been handed down for generations. There are special areas that have meaning to the entire tribal group, places that figure prominently in origin stories, places that have religious meaning, and places that mark tribal "boundaries."

So why is there a need for tribes to "reclaim" their physical heritage in terms of sacred sites? There are many reasons, but the primary one relates to the ways that tribes have lost control over their ancestral homelands—and the most common way that tribes have lost their land is through treaties.

TREATIES

Historically, the formal U.S. governmental relationship with American Indians has primarily been established through treaties. Treaties are formal agreements between separate governments. Today, you might hear about disarmament treaties, where separate nations sign an agreement that says they will do away with certain classes of weapons. In the early days of U.S. history, when the United States was still a small country, the government entered into treaties with the Indian tribes. These treaties helped the United States gain land, friendship, and allies in some of its early wars, and established the idea that the tribes were separate nations with which the government had to deal.

In general, the relationships between the United States and Indian tribes were good, although there were problems, as there are among all nations. But with the continued westward movement of American citizens into new lands, a growing conflict developed over Indian rights. As the population in the East grew, and, with it, the need for additional land to cultivate, the United States entered into more and more treaties with the tribes for land. The tribes signed treaties whereby they agreed to give up tracts of land in exchange for promises of protection, for money, and for other lands in the West.

With the discovery of gold in the Southeast, the Cherokees found themselves in the middle of a fight between the governments of the United States and the State of Georgia. In Georgia, Samuel J. Worcester, a missionary residing on Cherokee lands, was placed in a Georgia jail for refusing to take an oath of allegiance to the state and for failing to obtain a permit from the state to allow him to reside in Cherokee country.

Worcester took his case all the way to the U.S. Supreme Court, and, in 1832, the Court decided in his favor, arguing that the Cherokees (and all Indian tribes, by extension) were sovereign nations that were not under the jurisdiction of the states. The decision, written by Chief Justice John Marshall, was important in that it established the concept that American Indians were "domestic dependent nations"—separate nations that exist within the borders of the United States but rely upon the U.S. government for particular benefits.

This decision should have been enough to establish a firm relationship between the states and Indian tribes, but the president of the United States at the time, Andrew Jackson, supported the State of Georgia over the Supreme Court. He has been quoted as saying in response to Marshall's decision: "John Marshall has made his decision. Now let him enforce it."[14]

Without support from the executive branch of the U.S. government, the State of Georgia continued to try to tax the Cherokees and to control Indians. Because of continuing problems in the state, the tribe decided to move from their homeland to Indian Territory, west of the Mississippi River. Because the tribal members numbered into the thousands, the tribe was expecting to migrate westward in stages. With the discovery of gold on Cherokee lands, however, the process was sped up. In the autumn of 1838, the U.S. Army rounded up the Cherokees and placed them in camps to begin their journey. Some Cherokees escaped the roundup and fled into the Smoky Mountains of Tennessee and North Carolina. Ultimately, they were granted a small reservation there.

The trip from Georgia to Indian Territory was undertaken in the winter of 1838–1839. The groups of Cherokees forced to march west were poorly supplied. Nearly one-fourth of the Cherokees who left Georgia died along the way, leading survivors to refer to the trek as "The Trail Where They Cried," also known as "The Trail of Tears."

Many other tribes were forced out of their homelands to faraway places in Indian Territory. Most of the tribes that once lived in the Northeast were moved farther and farther west until they ultimately ended up in Indian Territory. In the Southeast, the Choctaws, Chickasaws, Creeks, and Seminoles, like the Cherokees, were removed to the Indian Territory, too, giving up their homes, farms, and businesses.

During the remainder of the 1800s, Indian tribes continued to be pushed to the limits of American "civilization." They signed treaty after treaty, each agreement promising to protect their new lands and their boundaries. Treaty after treaty was soon broken for one reason or another. By the end of the 1800s, Indian tribes no longer had access to all the land that was once theirs. Often, treaties established "reservations," where specific land was set aside for tribes. These reservations were generally smaller than the lands that the tribes were accustomed to living on, and their ability to freely move about was diminished so much that they no longer could visit their important tribal sites or the places where their ancestors were buried.

SACRED PLACES AND FEDERAL LAW

More and more land that had once been shared by everyone soon became the private property of individuals or families, but some of the most remarkable geography in the West was retained by the U.S. government and has found its way into the National Park System for the enjoyment of all citizens of the United States. Places like the Black Hills of South Dakota, the Yosemite Valley of northern California, Yellowstone in Wyoming and Montana, and Devils Tower in Wyoming are treasured for their natural beauty and their recreational uses. Places such as the Grand Canyon are valued because of their untamed, natural state, while others like the Pipestone Quarries of Minnesota are important because of the natural resources found there.

All these places are held in trust for all Americans by the U.S. government because of their uniqueness. But to American Indians, these areas have more meaning than just their beauty or their recreational uses. Some are places of tribal origin, sites linked to tribal history, or places that served as refuge in times of conflict. These areas have special, sacred meaning to Indian tribes.

Nearly all tribes in the United States attach some importance to places within the landscapes that they inhabit or previously inhabited. As various authors have noted, one of the main tenets in the Native American belief system is the idea that spiritual power is spread throughout the environment in

The U.S. government holds some Native sacred places in trust, such as this area in California, which, under the Native American Sacred Lands Act, was deemed sacred by the federal government in July 2002. Shown here is California Senator Barbara Boxer, who is displaying the site of a proposed gold mine.

general, although there are interconnected special places that form an intersection between the physical and spiritual worlds. These places can be found throughout the universe and are infused with "power," which helps people achieve good health, good luck, and good energy. "Power" can be defined as a sort of spiritual energy or life force that enables an individual to interact with the forces of the natural and supernatural worlds. It can be obtained by people who know how to gather it from sacred places, for example, vision quest sites, resource gatherings sites, sweat lodge sites, and burial sites.

What are "sacred places"? The answer to a question such as this seems obvious to most Americans, but the definition is actually very complex. For example, anthropologist Jane Hubert points out that "what makes something sacred to people of a different culture may have none of the characteristics or trappings of those things or places they consider sacred in their own society."[15] Sacred places may be many things. To an American, Gettysburg is a special place because it is the site of a major battle during the Civil War (1861–1865), where a large number of people were killed. It has very special meaning to citizens of the United States, but it would not likely be considered "sacred." Is an abandoned church in your hometown always sacred, or is it sacred only when it is being used as a church for religious purposes? Are all parts of the church sacred or just the main room? Is a church kitchen or nursery sacred? Are church bathrooms sacred?

Among American Indians, the idea of a sacred site carries with it more than just the idea of a place's physical characteristics or its location on the landscape. When an area is considered sacred, a person's relationship with that place changes. There are unwritten rules and regulations that govern an individual's behavior at the site. There are also sets of beliefs about the place, beliefs often associated with spiritual beings, whether they are spirits of the ancestors or more powerful gods or spirits. There is also a relationship between the sacred space and the profane or mundane space around it.

One law that relates to the protection of historic properties in the United States is also important in protecting sacred places. The National Historic Preservation Act of 1966 requires governmental agencies to look for historic properties that might be affected by government actions such as construction, earthmoving, or any sort of land modification. These properties might be buildings of a certain style or construction; archaeological or historical sites of importance to local, regional, or national groups; properties of importance that relate to a specific historical individual; or properties that reflect the work of an architectural master. Of these properties, one type protected by this law is called a "traditional cultural property."

A traditional cultural property is defined as a property that is associated with the cultural practices or beliefs of a living community that are rooted in that community's history and are essential to maintaining the continuing cultural identity of the community. The relationship of these properties to the landscape of which they are a part is perhaps as important as the actual property itself.

While federal agencies must identify historic properties that might be affected by a particular undertaking, most properties associated with Native American groups are by their very nature difficult for non-tribal members to recognize for their spiritual, rather than purely historical, value. Because these sites have special meaning to members of American Indian communities, the nature of sacred sites themselves may be very different and difficult for those outside of the culture to appreciate. What makes something sacred to people of one culture may have none of the characteristics or trappings of those things or places that others consider sacred in their own society. Additional problems associated with recognizing traditional cultural properties include identifying the tribal groups native to the area and developing a framework for understanding whether or not a traditional cultural property even exists. A cluster of rocks may appear to a non-Indian to be little more than that, but a tribal member might recognize the rocks' placement as an indication that a sweat lodge is present. A collection of deer skulls with antlers might be a hunting shrine; a mountaintop that might not have any indications of cultural use might actually hold a very important place in the *cosmology* (the belief system that deals with the universe) of a tribal group.

Access to Sacred Sites

As mentioned earlier, many (if not most) of the sites sacred to tribal groups are no longer within lands owned or controlled by the tribes. To get to sacred sites on privately owned lands, tribal members often have to ask special permission of the landowners, and they may or may not be granted access. If a sacred site exists on city, county, or state lands, access may be allowed, but the access might only be granted during regular "business hours" or at times when the area is crowded with lots of other people. On lands under the ownership or control of the federal government, however, there is a special allowance made for tribal access to special areas. Unfortunately, as Nicole Price, the director of Medicine Wheel Alliance (MWA), a multiracial group of Native American practitioners and environmentalists, points out: "(W)hen a sacred site is part of a federal, state, or local property, it usually becomes a tourist attraction for the area. This may be the reason why Native American Indians are reluctant to discuss or identify areas of importance."[16]

On May 24, 1996, President Bill Clinton issued Executive Order 13007, which dealt with American Indian sacred sites. An executive order is not a law, but it is procedural guideline that requires specific action by all federal agencies. Executive Order 13007 required that each executive branch agency with statutory or administrative responsibility for the management of federal lands accommodate access to and ceremonial use of sacred sites by Indian religious practitioners and avoid adversely affecting the physical integrity of such sacred sites. Where appropriate, agencies were charged with maintaining the confidentiality of sacred sites identified in response to the order. The order defined a sacred site as a "specific, discrete, narrowly delineated location on federal land that is identified by an Indian tribe, or Indian individual determined to be an appropriately authoritative representative of an Indian religion, as sacred by virtue of its established religious significance to, or ceremonial use by, an Indian religion."[17]

Indian tribes were supposedly assured access to sacred sites once they identified the sites' location to the federal agency on whose land the sites were located, provided that the accommodation of the religious use of the area was not clearly inconsistent with essential agency functions, such as military training.

Four Examples of Sacred Places

The Four Sacred Mountains

In Navajo cosmology, there are four sacred mountains that form the boundaries of their traditional world in the southwestern United States. Navajo stories tell of the sacred mountains and their roles in the Navajo way of life.

The sacred mountain of the east, Mount Blanca in southeastern Colorado, is represented by the color white and symbolizes the morning of the day, as well as the morning of life. White shell is associated with this direction.

The sacred mountain of the south is Mount Taylor in northwestern New Mexico, and is associated with the color blue and the gemstone turquoise. The color blue represents knowledge, wealth, and well-being.

The sacred mountain of the west is San Francisco Peak in northeastern Arizona, and is associated with the color yellow. Yellow represents the family hearth and the power of the family. Abalone shell is associated with this direction.

Finally, the sacred mountain of the north is Mount Hesperus in southern Colorado. Black is the color of the direction and it is associated with the night. Black jet is the gem associated with this direction.

The four sacred mountains mark the boundaries of the traditional world of the Navajos, not only in a geographical sense, but also in a philosophical sense. The mountains teach the Navajos about place and relationships not only with the external world but also within their inner person. By viewing these sacred places, the Navajos are reminded of the spiritual journey they undertake daily and over the course of their lifetimes, and the need to maintain a balance with nature, with others, and with themselves.

Mount Taylor, depicted here in a nineteenth-century sketch, is sacred to the Navajos. The mountain, which is located in northwestern New Mexico, is one of four sacred mountains that form the boundaries of the Navajo homeland.

Bear Butte

Bear Butte, near Sturgis, South Dakota, is a butte (a steep-sided hill) on the grassland prairie of the northern Great Plains. Every year, thousands of American Indians climb a trail from the bottom of the butte, beginning in a South Dakota state park parking lot, and wind their way up to the top of the butte. At the top, the view is remarkable, with the vast ocean of prairie grasses to the north, east, and south, and the sacred Black Hills to the west. Also at the top, American Indians leave spiritual offerings, offer prayers for friends and loved ones, and make spiritual connections to all the other Indians who have visited this sacred site.

Crazy Horse, the great Lakota warrior, was said to have been born near Bear Butte. Bear Butte itself is a place where many American Indians have participated in sweat lodge ceremonies and vision quests. A vision quest is an intense time of solitude and fasting that is often undertaken by Indian youth on the verge of adulthood. During the time of hunger and solitude, visions often appear to the youth. This vision, when interpreted by a tribal medicine person, was thought to foretell the future of the individual.

Bear Butte today is a South Dakota state park, and every year, thousands of Indian and non-Indian visitors climb a rocky pathway to the top. Along the pathway, pieces of red cloth tied to tree limbs mark places where people have offered prayers. Although these prayers are important to tribal people, many non-Indians remove these pieces of cloth out of ignorance, misunderstanding, or a mistaken belief that they have been forgotten. In addition, many non-Indians tie red cloth strips to trees in an attempt to practice the Plains way of praying. Though this might be considered a sincere form of flattery, tribal members often see it as an inconsiderate act. To them, Bear Butte is sacred for Indians, and any non-Indian use of the area is sacrilegious.

Bear Butte is a place of power for individual Indians and for the Indian tribes that hold it sacred. It is a place where tribal people have gone to receive power for more than 150 years. It is a place to be respected and revered. It is not worshiped as a place of power but it is sacred because of the power that resides there.

Bear Lodge

Bear Lodge/Devils Tower is an imposing site near Hulett, in northeastern Wyoming. A granite plug rising more than 860 feet from its base to its top, Devils Tower was made famous by the 1977 science-fiction movie *Close Encounters of the Third Kind* as an otherworldly apparition in the middle of nowhere. It is a place where rock climbers challenge their skill and strength against some difficult rock climbing routes, but it is also a place that is sacred to more than twenty Indian tribes. The site was named Devils Tower by a scientific team in 1875, but many Indian tribes call it "Bear Lodge." One of these tribes, the Kiowa of Oklahoma, has a story about how it came into being.

The story goes that, one day long ago, eight children were playing—seven sisters and their brother. Suddenly, the boy was struck by some sort of magic and began to tremble and run on all fours. His hands and feet became claws and his body became covered with fur. After the transformation was completed, a bear stood where the boy had been, and he began to chase the girls.

The girls ran to a tree trunk, and the tree told them to climb onto it. As the bear approached to try to kill the girls, the tree trunk began to rise higher and higher into the sky. The bear tried to get the girls and clawed at the tree trunk, scratching it on all sides and leaving claw marks all over it. The girls were carried all the way up into the sky, where they became the seven stars of the Big Dipper; the tree trunk became the mountain. Visitors, say the Indians, can still see the bear's claw marks on the sides of the mountain.

Thus, while the tower is considered a favorite place of recreation for climbers, it has special significance and sacred meaning to the Kiowas and other tribes. Today, rock climbers are asked not to climb the tower during the month of June, when many tribal people participate in vision quests at the park. The climbing ban is not enforced by the National Park Service—to close the park to climbers for American Indian religious reasons would possibly jeopardize the constitutionally required separation between church and state, but the climbers are asked to respect American Indian wishes and perspectives about the tower as a sacred location.

American Indians view the rock climbers who use the tower for sport as equivalent to someone who might choose to climb a cathedral or a church. Do the Indians have a point? Should this sacred place be closed to rock climbers all the time or perhaps for one month out of the year?

Nanih Waiya

In Neshoba County, Mississippi, there is a mound of dirt that is called *Nanih Waiya*, the "mother mound" of the Choctaw tribe. It is seen as the spiritual place that is the point of origin of the Muscogee (Creek), Cherokee, Chickasaw, and Choctaw tribes of the southeastern United States.

A Choctaw origin story tells that a group of people came out of a hole in Nanih Waiya, lay on the ground until they were dry, then got up and walked to the east. They crossed a river and camped on the other side. After staying there for a short while, they traveled farther east until they found a spot that was to their liking. These people became the Creeks.

A second group came out of the mound and lay about on the ground until they were dry, then followed the path of the previous group to the east. They crossed the river and saw the ashes from the fires that the first group had built. They started east again, but soon got lost and turned north. These people became the Cherokees.

A third group came out of the mound and lay on the ground until they were dry. They followed the trail of the first two groups and got to the river. They saw the campfires on the opposite side of the river but decided not to go any farther. Instead, they settled where they were. These people became the Chickasaws.

Finally, a fourth group came out of the mound. They lay on the side of the mound until they were dry and saw the path that the three previous groups had taken. Instead of walking on the same pathway the others had taken, however, the people looked around, saw that they were already in a wonderful place, and decided to remain where they were. These people became the Choctaws.

The mound Nanih Waiya is marked by a sign in a small park near the Pearl River Reservation of the Mississippi Band of Choctaw in Mississippi, and is still a sacred area to both the Mississippi Band of Choctaw and the Choctaw Nation of

Oklahoma. Did the southeastern tribes of Indians *really* come out of a hole in the mound? Perhaps not, but is the Choctaw tribe's story truly more difficult to believe than the biblical story of the Garden of Eden? How sacred would the Garden of Eden be if it were found?

Summary

American Indian tribes have a long-standing relationship with the geography that was once within their home ranges but now predominantly lies outside of the areas within tribal control. Throughout their time in North America, Indians have ascribed religious meaning to special areas for their appearance, for their relationship to creation stories, for their use as an area where power might be obtained, or for their connection to other aspects of tribal cosmology. U.S. citizens have often tried to prevent tribes from using these areas, or have displayed a remarkable callousness toward American Indian religious use of these areas. Devils Tower, for example, by its very name equates a Native sacred site with the personification of evil, Christianity's "devil."

You may have been to, or at least seen pictures of, Mount Rushmore in southwestern South Dakota. Mount Rushmore is located within the Black Hills, mountains that have sacred qualities to the Lakota tribe. Mount Rushmore is an example of the United States symbolically imposing its beliefs on American Indians. Carved into Mount Rushmore are the faces of four U.S. presidents. To Indians, these carvings represent Americans' power to place their brand on sacred lands. To some Indians, the carved mountain is like graffiti being scribbled on the National Cathedral in Washington, D.C., or a name spray-painted on the Vatican.

The American Indian relationship to sacred places is very much a part of a continuing religion. American Indians use these places as conduits for gaining personal and tribal power, as places where prayers are offered to spiritual beings that inhabit or visit the areas, and as places to come to an understanding of their own position within a larger world. With the passage of Executive Order 13007 in 1996, the U.S. government recognized the special relationship that Indians have to places, but the order only relates to procedures and access to sites on federally owned or controlled lands. It does not apply to private lands or to lands owned by state, county, or local governments.

Tribal governments are trying to hold on to traditional ways of living and practicing their religions, and places on the landscape are an important part of this maintenance. Until tribal groups are able to gain free access to their sacred areas without outside interference or observation, their religion will continue to be constrained.

In addition, it becomes important that the federal government works with state and local governments to enact laws that can adequately protect such places. Some people find it difficult to picture a mountain or a river as being sacred—as sacred as a church or a synagogue. But many American Indian religions hold such places as important and sacred and the Constitution of the United States requires the government to protect them.

8

Conclusions and Hopes for the Future

The previous pages have only scratched the surface of the history that underlies the issues that face American Indians and anthropologists as they work to find a middle ground. Anthropologists feel that their contributions to the history of humanity from its inception until the present provide sufficient reasons for their continuing research; professional curiosity is another reason, of course, but curiosity has always made humans strive harder and reach further.

We have discussed the history of the relationship between Euro-Americans and American Indians and have also looked at how American Indians have been portrayed in anthropological literature. Are Indians still being depicted in the same ways, or are they now being treated as equals?

Social scientists, in general, are trying to change anthropology into a discipline that not only takes into account the wishes of descendant populations in its research, but also one that tries to work with descendant groups to conduct studies that will be beneficial to modern communities. Anthropologists are trying to answer questions that the communities want answered in order to demonstrate the utility of their research. They are also trying to stop being outsiders—"objective," unfeeling, and all-recording scientists.

At the same time, archaeologists are trying to find ways to better include American Indian wishes in their discipline. They are trying to change the way they view the past. Rather than the traditional perspective that the past and all associated with it is the exclusive "property" of the scientist, they are attempting to recognize that the true implications of ownership and the ability to share the interpretation and modeling of the past should be equally shared. How long it will take to firmly establish a discipline that shares and appreciates alternate ways of viewing, reporting, and interpreting the past is unknown, but there are some archaeologists who have already begun to chart the path toward that goal.

The influence of the past is always with us. Just because something happened "before now" or "before today" does not mean it is gone. All time interconnects with all other points in time. There would be no "today" without the presence of the past and the promise of the future. Think about it: All our yesterdays are still connected to the person we are right at this moment. The person we will be tomorrow is interconnected with the person we were last year. All the world's different cultures are likewise interwoven.

Is there a future for museums? Is there a need for places that some see as paying homage to the items of those whose lives were lived out in the culture of "long ago"? Are museums graveyards for dead objects, storage crypts for dusty skeletons, or mausoleums for extinct cultures? The future of museums lies in our hands, to an extent. If you can see the utility for them, they will continue to exist as institutions that exhibit special objects, which can help teach about the ways cultures adapted to their

During the late nineteenth and early twentieth centuries, many archaeologists took cultural objects from southwestern Indian tribes, including the Pueblo. Shown here is Dr. Rubie Watson, the director of the Peabody Museum of Archaeology and Ethnology at Harvard University, who is returning cultural objects to Raymond Gachupin, governor of the Pueblo of Jemez, and Ruben Sando, governor of the Pueblo of Pecos, in 1999.

environments in earlier times. They can offer us insights into the people we were "back then." But they can't exist unless we continue to give them life—either in books, in our memories, or in our daily lives. Museums cannot exist just for the sake of existing; they require a purpose.

The conflict regarding the repatriation of human remains, grave goods, sacred objects, and items of cultural patrimony is ongoing, but it may lessen in the future if both American Indians and anthropologists can come to terms about the issues that underlie the conflict. The history that the two groups share is checkered, but that history does not need to be repeated again and again.

The way anthropologists and other scientists view

American Indian skeletal material has changed since the 1970s. Things have changed as our society rethought its treatment of Native dead in recent years. We have stopped thinking of skeletons as "property," or resources to be mined. More and more it is being remembered that they once were people, and we all have responsibilities to treat them with the respect they deserve. In the 1980s, Native people sought social change in order to obtain the same legal protections that the United States gives to the graves and dead of other races.

American Indian culture cannot exist as it once did. Today, it is a mixture of remembered traditions, cherished ceremonies, and relatively new relationships with other groups. No one can live in the past, nor can a culture go back to where it was years ago. American Indian tribes have continued to adapt to the present and to grow into cultures that are alive and breathing. Yet they still maintain an understanding of the important things that made them into the cultures that currently exist: tradition and relationships with the past.

Sacred lands and sacred sites help tie American Indian cultures to the earth and act as anchors for the present culture to hold on to. Sacred land is an easy concept to understand but a tough one to put into practice. With constantly expanding urban areas, recreational places, and resource exploitation, land is more and more in demand. Access to places becomes ever more difficult for those who wish to regain their connection to the land, and private property owners—while they might understand the need for spiritual connection to particular places—eventually grow leery when too many individuals try to gain access to areas of their property.

Government attempts at access are well intended but often come at a price to many traditional individuals. For President Clinton's Executive Order 13007 to be effective in providing access to government land, an individual recognized as a spokesperson for the tribe must indicate the location of the sacred land that tribal members want to use. Many American

A growing concern for many American Indians is the intrusion of "New Age" groups on their sacred sites. Shown here is the Stone Lions Shrine at Bandelier National Monument in New Mexico—a sacred site to many Pueblos, but one that has recently been disturbed by New Age pilgrims who come to the site to experience a spiritual connection.

Indians are apprehensive about revealing the locations of sacred sites out of fear that these places will be made public. American Indians are also afraid of the "New Age" religions that have adopted tribal ceremonies and concepts into a non-Indian perspective in attempts to "find" the meaning of religion through the eyes of the Indian. Though these new religious practitioners may mean no harm, their imitation is considered sacrilegious.

Put yourself in the place of the Indian person who goes to visit a sacred site and must remove the objects put there by people trying to find their way into a religion that neither recognizes nor welcomes them. There are certain religions that welcome universal participation, but many of the traditional Native practices specifically exclude non-Indians.

At present, there are many other American Indian issues that may be more urgent than the ones discussed here. Issues such as health care, drug abuse, and illiteracy plague reservations and urban localities alike. Alcoholism is a leading killer, as is diabetes.

But American Indians aren't the only group that has to face these issues. Indigenous populations in other countries are generally among the poorest, most marginal populations. In industrialized countries in Scandinavia, the Saamis (once called "Laplanders") share social problems and stigma similar to those of American Indians. In New Zealand, the Maoris are regaining control of their heritage but still face obstacles. In Australia, the Aboriginal people are among the poorest educated, shortest lived, and most socially marginalized groups in the world.

Education and the promotion of cultural heritage will be vital in helping others understand the numerous attributes that make every culture different and special. For many American Indians, the protection of sacred sites and the repatriation of their cultural items will go a long way in helping to preserve their way of life.

1492 Christopher Columbus "discovers" the New World.

1520 Hernando Cortez "conquers" the Aztecs.

1539 Hernando de Soto explores the southeastern United States.

1620 Pilgrims land at Plymouth Rock, Massachusetts; first American Indian grave plundered.

1778 United States signs its first treaty with an Indian tribe—the Delaware.

1794 President Thomas Jefferson excavates an Indian mound.

1846 Smithsonian Institution established.

1862 U.S. Army Medical Museum requests "Indian specimens" to add to its collection of Indian crania.

1864 Cheyenne Indians massacred at Sand Creek, Colorado, by Colonel John Chivington and the Third Colorado Volunteers.

1868 United States signs a treaty with the Nez Perce, the last of its 370 treaties.

1894 American Indians accepted as builders of the moundworks of the east.

1899 Onondaga Nation sues John Boyd Thatcher for return of four wampum belts.

1906 Antiquities Act passed.

1909 New York State declared to be "wampum keeper."

1970 Taos Pueblo regains Blue Lake; Onondagas request return of wampum from New York State; Native American Rights Fund (NARF) founded.

1971 American Indians protest display of skeletons and sacred items at the Southwest Museum of the American Indian in Los Angeles, California.

1978 Congress passes the American Indian Religious Freedom Act.

1979 Congress passes the Archaeological Resources Protection Act.

1980 American Indians Against Desecration founded.

1981 Iowa passes first United States reburial law; American Association of Museums publishes ethical standards for treatment of Native American collections.

1987 Larsen Bay Tribal Council requests return of all Uyak site ancestral human remains and associated materials from Smithsonian.

1988 American Association of Museums publishes "Policy Regarding the Repatriation of Native American Ceremonial Objects and Human Remains."

1989 Onondagas regain wampum from New York State; Congress passes the National Museum of the American Indian Act.

1990 Congress passes the Native American Graves Protection and Repatriation Act.

1991 Smithsonian returns the human remains and associated objects to the Larsen Bay Tribal Council for reburial.

1993 Cheyennes rebury human skeletal remains from Sand Creek.

1996 Executive Order 13007 on Indian Sacred Sites. President Clinton issues statement in support of continued protection of Native American religious freedom and sacred sites.

2002 Congress passes Native American Sacred Lands Act.

Chapter 2:
Why Is There Conflict and What Is Repatriation?

1   Tex G. Hall, chairman, Three Affiliated Tribes of the Fort Berthold Indian Reservation, written submission, hearing before the Committee on Indian Affairs, United States Senate, One Hundred Sixth Congress, First Session, April 20, 1999, 79.

Chapter 3:
Repatriation Legislation

2   Jesse Taken Alive, written submission, Hearing before the Committee on Indian Affairs, United States Senate, One Hundred Fourth Congress, First Session, December 6, 1995: 231.

3   Lakota Holy Man Vernal Cross, as quoted by Larry Zimmerman in "'Tell Them about the Suicide': A Review of Recent Materials on the Reburial of Prehistoric Native American Skeletons," *American Indian Quarterly:* 333–343, Fall 1986.

4   Rob Bonnichsen, quote available online at *www.wweek.com/html/cover042298.html.*

5   Joseph B. Frazier, "Court: Scientists Can Study Kennewick Man," Associated Press, February 4, 2004. Available online at *http://www.cnn.com/2004/TECH/ science/02/05/kennewick.man.ap/*

Chapter 4:
Repatriation and Anthropology

6   Don Sampson, former Board of Trustees chairman for the Confederated Tribes of the Umatilla Indian Reservation, position paper dated November 21, 1997. Available online at *www.umatilla.nsn.us/kman2.html.*

7   Armand Minthorn, in a speech from October 27, 1996. Available online at *www.umatilla.nsn.us/kman1.html.*

8   Dorothy Lippert, "In Front of the Mirror: Native Americans and Academic Archaeology," *Native Americans and Archaeologists: Stepping Stones to Common Ground,* eds. Nina Swidler, Kurt E. Dongoske, Roger Anyon, and Alan S. Downer (Walnut Creek, Calif.: Almira Press, 1997), 126.

9   Jack F. Trope and Walter Echo-Hawk, "The Native American Graves Protection and Repatriation Act: Background and Legislative History," *Repatriation Reader: Who Owns American Indian Remains?* Ed. Devon A. Mihesuah (Lincoln, Nebr.: University of Nebraska Press, 2000), 151.

Chapter 5:
Repatriation and Museums

10   Marla Big Boy, an attorney for the Colville Tribe, as quoted in Coleman 12/11/98.

Chapter 6:
Summary of Repatriation Issues

11   Patricia Parker, "Traditional Cultural Properties: What You Do and How We Think," CRM, vol. 16, 1993, 5.

12   Ruthann Knudsen, "Archaeology and the Public." Available online at *www.cr.nps.gov/seac/protecting/html/ 1a-knudson.htm.*

Chapter 7:
Reclaiming Physical Heritage: Sacred Sites

13   Dorothy Theodoratus and Frank LaPena, "Wintu Sacred Geography of Northern California," *Sacred Sites, Sacred Places,* ed. D.L. Carmichael, J. Hubert, B. Reeves, and A. Schanche (London and New York: Routledge Press, 1997), 22.

14   Eric Foner and John A. Garraty, eds., *The Reader's Companion to American History* (Boston, Mass.: Houghton Mifflin Company), 160.

15   Jane Hubert, "Sacred Beliefs and Beliefs of Sacredness," *Sacred Sites, Sacred Places,* eds. D.L. Carmichael, J. Hubert, B. Reeves, and A. Schanche (London and New York: Routledge Press, 1997), 11.

16   Nichole Price, "Tourism and the Bighorn Medicine Wheel: How Multiple Use Does Not Work for Sacred Land Sites," *Sacred Sites, Sacred Places,* eds. D.L. Carmichael, J. Hubert, B. Reeves, and A. Schanche (London and New York: Routledge Press, 1997), 263.

17   Executive Order 13007, May 24, 1996. Available online at *www.cr.nps.gov/ local-law/eo13007.htm.*

Bibliography

American Anthropological Association Code of Ethics: *http://www.aaanet.org/committees/ethics/ethcode.htm*

American Association of Physical Anthropologists Code of Ethics, Second Draft: *http://www.physanth.org/positions/ethics.htm*

Ames, Michael M. *Cannibal Tours and Glass Boxes: The Anthropology of Museums.* Vancouver, B.C.: University of British Columbia Press, 1992.

Ashmore, Wendy, and Robert J. Sharer. *Discovering Our Past: A Brief Introduction to Archaeology*, 3rd ed. New York: Mayfield Press, 2000.

Bray, Tamara L., ed. *The Future of the Past: Archaeologists, Native Americans and Repatriation.* New York: Garland Publishing, 2001.

Brown, Dee. *Bury My Heart at Wounded Knee: An Indian History of the West.* New York: Holt, Rinehart, & Winston, 1970.

Buikstra, Jane. "A Specialist in Ancient Cemetery Studies Looks at the Reburial Issue." *Early Man* 3:26–27, 1980.

Carmichael, David L., Jane Hubert, Brian Reeves, and Audhild Schanche, eds. *Sacred Sites, Sacred Places.* New York: Routledge, 1997.

Clavir, Miriam. *Preserving What Is Valued: Museums, Conservation, and First Nations.* Vancouver, B.C.: University of British Columbia Press, 2002.

Coleman, Michael. "Tribes Want Remains Buried." *Albuquerque Journal,* December 11, 1998.

Downey, Roger. *Riddle of the Bones: Politics, Science, Race, and the Story of Kennewick Man.* New York: Copernicus Books, 2000.

Fagan, Brian. *Ancient North America: The Archaeology of a Continent*, 2nd ed. New York: Thames and Hudson, 1995.

Fine-Dare, Kathleen S. *Grave Injustice: The American Indian Repatriation Movement and NAGPRA.* Lincoln, Nebr.: University of Nebraska Press, 2003.

Frazier, Joseph B. "Court: Scientists Can Study Kennewick Man." Associated Press, February 4, 2004. Available online at *http://story.news.yahoo.com/news?tmpl=story&u=/ap/20040205/ap_on_sc/kennewick_man_2*

Goldstein, Lynne. "The Potential for Future Relationships between Archaeologists and Native Americans." *Ethics in American Archaeology,* edited by Mark J. Lynott and Alison Wylie, 2nd Rev. Ed. Society for American Archaeology, 2000.

Bibliography

Gulliford, Andrew. *Sacred Objects and Sacred Places: Preserving Tribal Traditions.* Boulder, Colo.: University of Colorado Press, 2000.

Hall, Tex G. Written submission, Native American Graves Protection and Repatriation Act: Hearing before the Committee on Indian Affairs, United States Senate, 106th Congress, First Session. April 20, 1999, 77–84.

Harrington, Spencer P.M. "Bones & Bureaucrats: New York's Great Cemetery Imbroglio." *Archaeology Magazine*, March/April 1993:29–38.

Heath, Dwight B., ed. *Mourt's Relation: A Relation or Journal of the English Plantation Settled at Plymouth in New England, by Certain English Adventurers both Merchants and Others.* Corinth Books, 1963.

Hinsley, Curtis. *The Smithsonian and the American Indian: Making a Moral Anthropology in Victorian America.* Washington, D.C.: Smithsonian Institution Press, 1981.

Hubert, Jane. "Sacred Beliefs and Beliefs of Sacredness." *Sacred Sites, Sacred Places,* edited by D.L. Carmichael, J. Hubert, B. Reeves, and A. Schanche. New York: Routledge Press, 1997.

Jones, D. Gareth, and Robyn J. Harris. "Archaeological Human Remains: Scientific, Cultural and Ethical Considerations." *Current Anthropology* 39:253–264, 1998.

Kehoe, Alice B. *America before the European Invasions.* New York: Pearson Education, Ltd., 2002.

Killion, Thomas W., and Tamara L. Bray. *Reckoning with the Dead: The Larsen Bay Repatriation and the Smithsonian Institution.* Washington, D.C.: Smithsonian Institution Press, 1994.

———, and Paula Molloy. "Repatriation's Silver Lining." *Working Together: Native Americans and Archaeologists,* edited by Kurt E. Dongoske, Mark Aldenderfer, and Karen Doehner, SAA, 2000.

Landau, Patricia M., and D. Gentry Steele. "Why Anthropologists Study Human Remains." *American Indian Quarterly* 20(2):209–228, 1996.

Lippert, Dorothy. "In Front of the Mirror: Native Americans and Academic Archaeology." *Native Americans and Archaeologists: Stepping Stones to Common Ground,* edited by Nina Swidler, Kurt E. Dongoske, Roger Anyon, and Alan S. Downer. Lanham, Md.: AltaMira Press, 1997.

Mihesuah, Devon, ed. *Natives and Academics: Researching and Writing about American Indians.* Lincoln, Nebr.: University of Nebraska Press, 1998.

———. *Repatriation Reader: Who Owns American Indian Remains?* Lincoln, Nebr.: University of Nebraska Press, 2000.

———. "American Indians, Anthropologists, Pothunters, and Repatriation: Ethical, Religious, and Political Differences." *American Indian Quarterly* 20(2):229–237, 1996.

NAGPRA Review Committee. *Recommendations Regarding the Disposition of Culturally Unidentifiable Native American Human Remains.* Available online at *http://www.cast.uark.edu/other/nps/nagpra/DOCS/rcrec004.html.*

———. *Draft Principles of Agreement Regarding the Disposition of Culturally Unidentifiable Human Remains.* Available online at *http://www.cast.uark.edu/other/nps/nagpra/DOCS/rcrec003.html.*

Naranjo, Tessie. Statement to the Committee. Native American Graves Protection and Repatriation Act: Hearing before the Committee on Indian Affairs, United States Senate, 104th Congress, First Session. December 6, 1995. Superintendent of Documents, 1996.

Nihipali, Kunani. Statement to the Committee. Native American Graves Protection and Repatriation Act: Hearing before the Committee on Indian Affairs, United States Senate, 104th Congress, First Session. December 6, 1995. Superintendent of Documents, 1996.

O'Hagan, Maureen. "Bones of Contention: The Agendas That Have Brought a 9,300 Year-Old Skeleton to Life." *Willamette Week*, April 22, 1998. Available online at *http://www.wweek.com/html/cover042298.html.*

Owsley, Douglas W., and Richard L. Jantz. "Archaeological Politics and Public Interest in Paleoamerican Studies: Lessons from Gordon Creek Woman and Kennewick Man." *American Antiquity* 66:565–575, 1998.

Parker, Patricia L. "Traditional Cultural Properties: What You Do and How We Think." *CRM* 16:1–5, 1993.

Price, Nichole. "Tourism and the Bighorn Medicine Wheel: How Multiple Use Does Not Work for Sacred Land Sites." *Sacred Sites, Sacred Places*, edited by D.L. Carmichael, J. Hubert, B. Reeves, and A. Schanche. New York: Routledge Press, 1997.

Prucha, Francis Paul. *Documents of United States Indian Policy*, 2nd Ed. Lincoln, Nebr.: University of Nebraska Press, 1990.

———. *American Indian Policy in the Formative Years.* Cambridge, Mass.: Harvard University Press, 1962.

Register of Professional Archaeologists Code. Available online at *http://www.rpanet.org/conduct.htm.*

Rose, Jerome C., Thomas J. Green, and Victoria D. Green. "NAGPRA Is Forever: The Future of Osteology and the Repatriation of Skeletons." *Annual Review of Anthropology* 25: 81–103, 1996.

Society for American Archaeology (SAA). *Principles of Archaeological Ethics.* Available online at *http://www.saa.org/publications/saabulletin/ 14-3/SAA9.html.*

Sprague, Roderick, and Walter W. Birkby. "Miscellaneous Columbia Plateau Burials." *Tebiwa* 13(1): 1–32, 1970.

Stapp, Darby C., and Michael S. Burney. *Tribal Cultural Resource Management: The Full Circle to Stewardship.* Lanham, Md.: AltaMira, 2002.

Taken Alive, Jesse. Written Submission, Native American Graves Protection and Repatriation Act: Hearing before the Committee on Indian Affairs, United States Senate, 104th Congress, First Session. December 6, 1995. Superintendent of Documents, 1996.

Theodoratus, Dorothea J., and Frank LaPena. "Wintu Sacred Geography of Northern California." *Sacred Sites, Sacred Places,* edited by D.L. Carmichael, J. Hubert, B. Reeves, and A. Schanche. New York: Routledge Press, 1997.

Thomas, David Hearst. *Skull Wars: Kennewick Man, Archaeology, and the Battle for Native American Identity.* New York: Basic Books, 2000.

Trigger, Bruce. "Prehistoric Archaeology and American Society: An Historical Perspective." *American Archaeology Past and Future,* edited by D.J. Meltzer, D.D. Fowler, and J. A. Sabloff. Washington, D.C.: Smithsonian Institution Press, 1986.

———. "Archeology and the Image of the American Indian." *American Antiquity* 45(4):662–676, 1980.

Trope, Jack F., and Walter Echo-Hawk. "The Native American Graves Protection and Repatriation Act: Background and Legislative History." *Repatriation Reader: Who Owns American Indian Remains?* Edited by Devon A. Mihesuah. Lincoln, Nebr.: University of Nebraska Press, 2000.

Ubelaker, Douglas, and Lauryn Guttenplan Grant. "Human Skeletal Remains: Preservation or Reburial?" *Yearbook of Physical Anthropology* 32:249–287. Alan R. Liss, Inc., 1989.

Watkins, Joe. *Indigenous Archaeology: American Indian Values and Scientific Practice.* Lanham, Md.: AltaMira, 2000.

Zimmerman, Larry. "'Tell Them about the Suicide': A Review of Recent Materials on the Reburial of Prehistoric Native American Skeletons." *American Indian Quarterly:* 333–343. Fall 1986.

———, and Brian Leigh Molyneaux. *Native North America.* Norman, Okla.: University of Oklahoma Press, 1996.

Books

Bray, Tamara L., ed. *The Future of the Past: Archaeologists, Native Americans and Repatriation.* New York: Garland Publishing, 2001.

Carmichael, David L., Jane Hubert, Brian Reeves, and Audhild Schanche, eds. *Sacred Sties, Sacred Places.* New York: Routledge, 1997.

Clavir, Miriam. *Preserving What Is Valued: Museums, Conservation, and First Nations.* Vancouver, B.C.: University of British Columbia Press, 2002.

Downey, Roger. *Riddle of the Bones: Politics, Science, Race, and the Story of Kennewick Man.* New York: Copernicus Books, 2000.

Fine-Dare, Kathleen S. *Grave Injustice: The American Indian Repatriation Movement and NAGPRA.* Lincoln, Nebr.: University of Nebraska Press, 2003.

Mihesuah, Devon, ed. *Repatriation Reader: Who Owns American Indian Remains?* Lincoln, Nebr.: University of Nebraska Press, 2000.

Thomas, David Hearst. *Skull Wars: Kennewick Man, Archaeology, and the Battle for Native American Identity.* New York: Basic Books, 2000.

Watkins, Joe. *Indigenous Archaeology: American Indian Values and Scientific Practice.* Lanham, Md.: AltaMira, 2000.

Websites

American Anthropological Association
   http://www.aaanet.org

About Archaeology
   http://archaeology.about.com

Archaeology Magazine
   http://www.archaeology.org

About NAGPRA
   http://www.cr.nps.gov/nagpra/

Kennewick Man History and Information, Tri-City Herald
   http://www.kennewick-man.com/

Society for American Archaeology
   http://www.saa.org

Films

In the Light of Reverence. A film directed by Christopher McLeod; produced by Christopher McLeod and Malinda Maynor. U.S. Release Date: 2001.

Index

Aborigines, 70
Age of Exploration, 55
Ahayu:da, 69, 70
Akwesasne Notes, 67
Alabama, 77–78
American Anthropological Association, 67
  on committee for American Indian reburial of remains, 19
American Association of Indian Affairs, 53
American Indian Movement (AIM), 12, 21
American Indian newspapers, 13–14
American Indian Religious Freedom Act (1978), 16, 21
American Indian remains, 2, 12, 15, 16, 28, 50, 51, 62–66, 102
  on private land, 79–81
  returning of, 4
  the study of and benefits to living people, 47–48
  treatment of, 19
American Indians Against Desecration, 21
American Museum of Natural History (New York), 42, 56, 61
  and run for profit, 57
American Science, 31
Ames, Michael, 56, 57
Anthropologists, 2, 10, 29
  and conflict with American Indians, 11–14
  and gathering information from human remains, 45–46
  on human skeletal material, 20
  and studying the American Indians remains, 42–43
Anthropology, 13–14
  and archaeology, 7, 13–14, 36
  on biological, 7, 42, 44, 46, 47, 51, 53, 73
  and cultural, 7
  definition of, 7, 35

on linguistic, 7
Archaeological Resources Protection Act of 1979 (ARPA), 80
Archaeologists, 2, 29, 36, 37, 79, 101
  and interest in Indian history, 39
Archaeology
  on digging into the past, 39
  meaning of, 36
  and sites, 38
Archaic period, 40
Arizona State Law Journal, 27
Army Medical Museum, 2
Artifacts, 2, 59–60, 79
  left at the site, 37
  value of, 69–70
Associated and unassociated funerary objects, 22
Attachment to place, 84
Australia, 70

Barnum, P.T., 56, 71
Bear Butte, 94–95
Bear Lodge, 95–96
Big Boy, Marla, 54
Black Hills (South Dakota), 88, 91
Bonnichsen, Rob, 31
Bureau of Indian Affairs (BIA), 77, 81
Bush, George H.W., 24

Caddo, 49
Chatters, James (Dr.), 29–30
Cherokees, 86
Cheyenne tribe (Oklahoma), 63, 64
Chicago Field Museum, 60, 73
Chivington, John M.,
Choctaw, 52, 97–98
Civil Rights, 11
Clinton, Bill, 92, 103
Close Encounters of the Third Kind (movie), 95
Collinsville, Illinois, 38
Columbia River, 29
Colville tribe, 33, 54
Context, 37

Index

Pearson, Maria, 20
Pilgrims, 1
Pipestone Quarries (Minnesota), 88
Policy for the disposition of Human
    Remains, 16, 62
Possession, 25
Powell, Joseph, 32
Price, Nicole, 92

Quapaw tribe, 49
Quivira, 41

Race, 31
Radiocarbon test, 30
Reburial Commission
  report of, 19
Receives federal funds, 25–26
Religion, 16, 19, 98–99
  the American Indians fight for, 4
Repatriation, 14, 34, 53, 69–71
  inadequacies of laws, 74–83
  meaning of, 35–36
  progress of, 82–83
  and support of, 21
Rose, Jerome, 32

Sacred objects, 22, 26–27, 73, 81, 102
Sacred places, 85, 103
  access to, 91–93
  examples of, 93
  and federal law, 88–91
Sampson, Don, 35
Sand Creek Massacre, 63, 65
San Francisco Peak, 93
Satanta's Shield, 81–82
Scientists, 36, 48, 50
Segregation, 11
Sioux tribe, 15
Skeletal morphology, 44–45, 103
Smith, Rob Roy, 33
Smithson, James, 56
Smithsonian Institution, 21–22, 23–25,
    52, 60, 63, 71
  and established, 56

on Larsen Bay, 65–66
on programs, 57
Social issues, 105
Social Scientists, 100–101
Society for American Archaeology,
    17–18
Society of Professional Archaeologists
  on proposal of a reburial policy, 18
Southwest Museum (Los Angeles), 12,
    60
  the protest, 68
Spiro Mounds, 38–39
Squanto, 1
Statement Concerning the Treatment
    of Human Remains, 17
Steele, D. Gentry, 44, 46, 62
Sun Dance, 4–5

Takings clause, 80
Tawakoni, 41
Texas, 20, 51
Thanksgiving, 1
Theodoratus, Dorothy, 84
Third Colorado Volunteers, 63
Thomas Burke Memorial Washington
    State Museum, 67
Traditional cultural property, 90, 91
Trail of Tears, 87
Treaties, 7, 11, 50, 87–88
  with the U.S. and the American
    Indians, 85–86
Tribal boundaries, 85
Tribal history, 88
Trigger, Bruce, 8
Trope, Jack, 53

Umatilla tribe, 31, 33
United States Corps of Engineers, 31
United States Court of Claims, 81
Uyak site, 65

Wampum belts, 67
Watertown Daily Times, 67
Welch (Minnesota), 12

Index

Westward expansion, 7
Wichita, 49
Worcester, Samuel J., 86
Writing, 39

Yellowman, Connie Hart, 65

Yellowstone National Park, 88
Yosemite Valley, 88

Zimmerman, Larry, 20
Zuni tribe, 66, 68–69, 70, 83

Joe Edward Watkins, Ph.D., a member of the Choctaw Nation of Oklahoma, is Associate Professor of Anthropology at the University of New Mexico. He has published a book, *Indigenous Archaeology: American Indian Values and Scientific Practice*, on the relationship between archaeologists/anthropologists and Native Americans and several articles on the same issue, including, "Archaeological Ethics and American Indians," which appears in *A Handbook for Ethics in Archaeology* and "Native Americans, Western Science, and NAGPRA," which appears in *Working Together: Native Americans & Archaeologists*.

Paul C. Rosier received his Ph.D. in American History from the University of Rochester, with a specialty in Native American History. His first book, *Rebirth of the Blackfeet Nation, 1912–1954*, was published by the University of Nebraska Press in 2001. In November 2003, Greenwood Press published *Native American Issues* as part of its Contemporary American Ethnic Issues series. Dr. Rosier has also published articles on Native American topics in the *American Indian Culture and Research Journal*, and the *Journal of American Ethnic History*. In addition, he was coeditor of *The American Years: A Chronology of United States History*. He is Assistant Professor of History at Villanova University, where he also serves as a faculty advisor to the Villanova Native American Student Association.

Walter Echo-Hawk is a member of the Pawnee tribe. He is a staff attorney of the Native American Rights Fund (*www.narf.org*) and a Justice on the Supreme Court of the Pawnee Nation (*www.pawneenation.org/court*). He has handled cases and legislation affecting Native American rights in areas such as religious freedom, education, water rights, fishing rights, grave protection, and tribal repatriation of Native dead.